Collins

Aiming for Level
Writing

5

Caroline Bentley-Davies

Gareth Calway

Robert Francis

Ian Kirby

Christopher Martin

Keith West

Series editor: Gareth Calway

William Collins' dream of knowledge for all began with the publication of his first book in 1819. A self-educated mill worker, he not only enriched millions of lives, but also founded a flourishing publishing house. Today, staying true to this spirit, Collins books are packed with inspiration, innovation and practical expertise. They place you at the centre of a world of possibility and give you exactly what you need to explore it.

Collins. Freedom to teach.

Published by Collins
An imprint of HarperCollins Publishers
77-85 Fulham Palace Road
Hammersmith
London
W6 8JB

Browse the complete Collins catalogue at
www.collinseducation.com

© HarperCollins Publishers Limited 2009

10 9 8 7 6 5 4 3 2
ISBN 978 0 00 731360 0

Caroline Bentley-Davies, Gareth Calway, Robert Francis, Ian Kirby, Christopher Martin and Keith West assert their moral rights to be identified as the authors of this work.

British Library Cataloguing in Publication Data.
A Catalogue record for this publication is available from the British Library.

Commissioning by Catherine Martin
Design and typesetting by Jordan Publishing Design
Cover Design by Angela English
Printed and bound by Printing Express, Hong Kong

With thanks to Sue Chapple, Chris Edge, Gemma Wain and Keith West.

Acknowledgements

The publishers gratefully acknowledge the permissions granted to reproduce the copyright material in this book. While every effort has been made to trace and contact copyright holders, where this has not been possible the publishers will be pleased to make the necessary arrangements at the first opportunity.

Extract from *Martyn Pig* by Kevin Brooks, reproduced by permission of The Chicken House (p14); extract from *The Power of Five: Raven's Gate* by Anthony Horowitz, © 2005 Anthony Horowitz, reproduced by permission of Walker Books Ltd, London SE11 5HJ (p21); extract from *Innsider (Brighton)*, reproduced by permission of Jury's Inn and Reputation Inc (p24); extract from an article in *The Sun*, 21 June 2008, reprinted by permission of NI Syndication (p25); Calvin & Hobbes cartoon © 1993 Watterson. Reprinted by permission of Universal Press Syndicate. All rights reserved (p28); cover of 'Get Active 4 Animals' leaflet reprinted by permission of Animal Aid (p32); extract from *Tribes* by Catherine Macphail, published by Puffin Books, part of The Penguin Group (p34); extracts from *Thursday's Child* by Sonya Hartnett, © 2000 Sonya Hartnett, reproduced by permission of Walker Books Ltd, London SE11 5HJ (pp40-1); extract from 'The Day I Fell Down the Toilet' by Steve Turner, published by Lion Hudson plc, 1996. Copyright © 1996 Steve Turner, used by permission of Lion Hudson plc (p48); extract from *A Handful of Dust* by Evelyn Waugh, reproduced by permission of The Penguin Group (p80).

The publishers would like to thank the following for permission to reproduce pictures in these pages.

Alamy (pp66, 71, 81); Alban Donohoe/Rex Features (p40); 'African slaves being taken on board ship bound for USA' Bridgeman Art Library (p6); Ashmolean Museum, University of Oxford/The Bridgeman Art Library (p12); Britainonview.com (p25t); Eliza Snow/istockphoto (p78); Getty Images (pp9, 24, 35t, 61); Heritage Images (p65); istockphoto (pp10,11,13, 15, 21, 23, 25b, 31, 35b, 43, 46, 47, 48, 52, 67, 77, 81r); James Steidly/istockphoto (p84); Jeremy Craine/Rex Features (p59); Mary Evans Picture Library (p70); Nils Jorgensen/Rex Features (p55); Photofusion Picture Library/Alamy (p45); Pictorial Press Ltd/Alamy (p20); Rex Features (p18); Rita Jacobs/istockphoto (p57); Ronald Grant Archive (p56); Time Life Pictures/Mansell/Getty Images (p37).

Contents

Chapter 1

AF1 Write imaginative, interesting and thoughtful texts

This chapter is going to show you how to

- Capture your reader's interest and imagination
- Choose the right type of text
- Plan, develop and shape your writing
- Write vividly, powerfully, precisely
- Develop a clear and convincing voice.

What's it all about?

Whatever you are writing, it is important to choose the right ideas and develop them in ways that will appeal to and interest your readers.

Capture your reader's interest and imagination

This lesson will
- show you how to bring your writing to life with imaginative detail.

When someone has something **interesting** or **exciting** to say, everyone listens. It's the same with writing – you must **interest your reader** and **capture their imagination**.

The poet John Keats said that when he watched a sparrow, he felt himself 'pick about the gravel' with the bird. To write well, you need to **imagine** well.

Getting you thinking

What would it be like to be violently kidnapped, and never see your home again? Read this account by Olaudah Equiano, an Igbo boy born in 1745, who was kidnapped into slavery at the age of 11. Here, after many months travelling as a prisoner, he reaches the sea:

Olaudah Equiano

> The first object which **saluted** my eyes when I arrived on the coast was the sea, and a slave ship. These filled me with astonishment, which was soon **converted** to terror. When I was carried on board, I was immediately handled, and tossed up to see if I were sound by some of the crew; and I was now persuaded that I had gotten into a world of bad spirits, and that they were going to kill me. When I looked round the ship too, and saw a large furnace of copper boiling, and a multitude of black people chained together, every one of their **countenances** expressing **dejection** and sorrow, I no longer doubted of my fate, and, quite overpowered with horror and **anguish**, I fell motionless on the deck and fainted.

Glossary

saluted: met
converted: turned
countenances: faces
dejection: sadness or hopelessness
anguish: worry

Top tips

Look for strong nouns and powerful verbs that create a vivid picture of the scene and describe the experience in a way that you can 'see'.

- With a partner, pick out **five details** that help you to imagine Olaudah's experience. Now join with another pair to compare and discuss your choices.

How does it work?

The writer describes what he could see so that the reader can **experience it through his eyes**. He shares his feelings (terror, horror, anguish) and expresses **how it seemed to him at the time**. ('I had gotten into a world of bad spirits'.)

Now you try it

Imagine you have been kidnapped and taken prisoner on this slave ship. Write an account describing your experiences as you are taken on board and the ship sets sail into the unknown.

Start by jotting down the details you could include in your writing. Including all the senses helps to create vivid writing. Think about

- what you can see (*the chains, the rats, the other slaves*)
- what you can hear (*the sailors yelling at you in a language you don't understand*)
- what you can smell (*the suffocating smells of the people cramped together*)
- what your thoughts and feelings are (*fear, terror, misery?*).

Development activity

Research the topic further and find out some more facts that you could include in your account. For example, use the internet to find out what slave ships looked like and what the conditions were like for the prisoners below deck.

Think about how you could improve your account by including these details. Can you describe these new details in a way that makes your reader 'see' them?

Check your progress	LEVEL 4	I can choose the right things to write about
	LEVEL 5	I can include imaginative details in my writing
	LEVEL 6	I can write and imagine in convincing detail

This lesson will
- show you how to write in a form that fits your purpose.

Choosing the right type of text means that you **think about the purpose of your writing and the audience first**. Then you choose **the appropriate form of writing to match**.

Getting you thinking

After he bought his freedom, Olaudah Equiano wrote an **autobiography** about his years of slavery called *The Interesting Narrative*. He wanted to persuade his readers to support the abolition (banning) of the slave trade.

What **other kinds of writing** might he have chosen to convince his readers to support him?

With a partner, look at the list below and put them in order of effectiveness. Discuss why you made your choices.

- *an angry letter to a newspaper*
- *a persuasive speech to Parliament*
- *an argumentative essay about the negative effects of slavery*
- *a poem expressing the suffering of slaves*
- *a leaflet or newsletter to support the campaign.*

How does it work?

All five forms of writing could be used to influence people against slavery:

- A speech to Parliament would directly try to influence the MPs who have the power to abolish the slave trade.
- An argumentative essay or campaigning leaflet might change the minds of the general public.
- An angry letter or a poem might have more emotional impact, helping people understand the cruelty of slavery.

Now you try it

Choose one of the forms of writing listed opposite and create a text to persuade readers to support the banning of the slave trade. You could use ideas from the poem 'The Sorrows of Yamba', by Hannah More, to help you.

Then for love of filthy Gold,
Strait they bore me to the sea;
   Cramm'd me down a Slave Ship's hold,
Where were Hundreds stow'd like me...

   At the savage Captain's beck,
Now like Brutes they make us prance;
   Smack the **Cat** about the Deck,
And in scorn they bid us dance.

   Nauseous horse beans they bring nigh,
Sick and sad we cannot eat;
   Cat must cure the Sulks they cry,
Down their throats we'll force the **meat**....

   Driven like Cattle to a fair,
See they sell us young and old;
   Child from Mother too they tear,
All for love of filthy Gold...

Glossary

Cat: a kind of whip
Nauseous: sickening
meat: any form of food

Top tips

You may want to explore web-based texts as a way to reach your audience. What, apart from writing, could you include in a website?

Development activity

Now think about how you could create a new piece of writing telling secondary school students today about the slave trade.

Choose the form of writing you think would be most effective to reach these readers. Then think about how you could adapt the information you have, to create this new text. Do you need to do any extra research?

Remember

- Your text must fit your purpose.
- Your language must fit the text.

Check your progress

LEVEL 4	I sometimes choose the best form for my writing
LEVEL 5	I can select and shape the most appropriate form for my writing to fit my purpose
LEVEL 6	I can develop the features of the form of writing I have chosen

This lesson will
● show you how to write from a plan.

Your writing will be much better if you **plan your approach** and **consider your structure** first. Make sure that you plan your writing in a way that helps you to **record the right ideas** and **organise them in the most effective way** to suit your purpose.

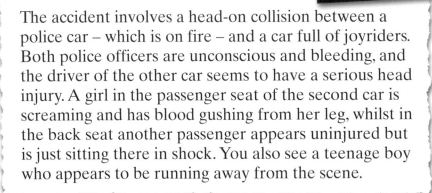

Getting you thinking

Imagine you are a police officer who has been called to the scene of a car crash. When you arrive, this is what you see:

> The accident involves a head-on collision between a police car – which is on fire – and a car full of joyriders. Both police officers are unconscious and bleeding, and the driver of the other car seems to have a serious head injury. A girl in the passenger seat of the second car is screaming and has blood gushing from her leg, whilst in the back seat another passenger appears uninjured but is just sitting there in shock. You also see a teenage boy who appears to be running away from the scene.

1   With a partner, role-play a conversation over the police radio between the police officer on the scene and the radio operator at the police station.

Think about what key information needs to be given and in what order.

What questions would the radio operator ask?

2   Now plan the official report of the incident that the police officer has to write on his or her return to the station. Think about which of these formats would be the most useful for planning a report:

- flow-chart
- spider diagram
- table or chart
- bullet-point list
- numbered list
- another choice of your own.

How does it work?

Sometimes we need to give and get information very quickly. In the role-play, you might have given the information about the fire first – requesting a fire engine to deal with the blaze – or about the most seriously injured people, asking for an ambulance.

However, in planning your report, a **flow-chart** or **bullet-point list** would help you to organise the information about the incident in the order in which it occurred.

Now you try it

Now you need to develop your plan before you draft your report of the accident. You will need to write a clear factual report, but also include a closing statement about which driver you believe caused the accident.

You could develop your plan by adding the following details to it:

- *a description of where the accident took place*
- *statements from witnesses about what they saw*
- *statements from the policemen involved in the accident*
- *statements from the passengers in the other car*
- *any other details that you noticed when you arrived at the scene.*

Your plan will help you organise and order the information in your report.

Top tips

Be logical. Organise your writing in the clearest way to get your point across.

- What point do you want to get across to your reader?
- Who is the reader?
- How will this reader best receive the message?

Remember

Report writing is **factual** writing; all the relevant facts must be included and all unnecessary information left out. This is not the time to show off your poetic talent or skills at narrative description! Keep it concise and official.

Development activity

Draft your report following the plan you have made. Remember that your opinion on who caused the accident must come at the **end** of the report, after you have built up the facts of the case.

This lesson will
- show you how to express strong feelings in sharp images.

Writing vividly and powerfully means making **imaginative word choices** to create an image in your reader's mind. You also need to **write precisely**, keeping your writing in **sharp focus** and avoiding vagueness or rambling.

Getting you thinking

Have you ever wished you could just draw what you mean, instead of having to find the right words? Make quick pencil sketches of what you mean by these words:

- loudmouth
- bighead.

Read these two poems and draw the images they create in your mind:

A

A touch of cold in the Autumn night –
I walked **abroad**
And saw the **ruddy** moon lean over a hedge
Like a red-faced farmer.

Glossary

abroad: outside in the oper
ruddy: red or pink

B

Whirl up, sea –
whirl your pointed pines,
splash your great pines
on our rocks,
hurl your green over us,
cover us with your pools of fir.

- Compare your drawings with a partner's.
- Do you think B is a description of the sea compared to a forest, or a forest compared to the sea?

Now you try it

Think of someone that you have very powerful feelings about – positive or negative. It can't be anyone in the room and you must keep the person's identity secret.

Now imagine them as a piece of furniture. What would they be?

- *A battered but very comfortable old armchair*
- *A sleek leather sofa with adjustable footrest*
- *A hard plastic stool?*

With a partner, take it in turns to describe the person you have chosen by answering these questions:

- What type of movement would this person be?
  (*the curl of the wind on the surface of a wave…*)
- What season would this person be?
  (*a cold windy autumn with damp and dying leaves crackling underfoot…*)
- What time of day would this person be?
  (*the moment you just want to give up between last lesson and detention!*)

Development activity APP

Now create a poem about the person you have described, using the best images you have come up with.

Think about how you could develop your imaginative word choices. If you said this person would be 'winter', extend this metaphor by describing exactly what kind of winter they are…

A cruel, frosty winter biting your toes…

When you have done a first draft, review and revise your poem by

- cutting any unnecessary filler words or phrases
- changing the order of lines to focus the reader's attention
- dropping any weaker lines that don't add to the image.

Remember

A **simile** says that something is **like** something else. A **metaphor** just says that something **is** something else. Look back at the poems and try to find examples of both.

Remember

Keep the identity of the person described ABSOLUTELY PRIVATE.

Check your progress

LEVEL 4	I can develop some of my ideas in detail
LEVEL 5	I can choose and develop imaginative images
LEVEL 6	I can create and sequence striking images in my poem

This lesson will
● help you to choose and develop a narrative voice.

When you are writing fiction, you create the 'voice' that is telling the story. Stories are usually told either in the **first person** (*I listened carefully at the door…* or *We didn't wait to hear who was coming*) or the **third person** (*He listened carefully at the door… or They didn't wait to hear who was coming*).

Getting you thinking

Read this extract from the novel *Martyn Pig* by Kevin Brooks. Martyn is telling the story.

> I wasn't that worried when she didn't show up the following morning. Not at first anyway. Annoyed, maybe. But not worried. Alex was often late. She could never understand why it bothered me. 'I'm here now, aren't I?' she'd say. She was right, in a way. If you like someone enough, it doesn't matter how long they keep you waiting – as long as they turn up in the end, it's all right. I can't help it, though. I hate waiting for someone to turn up. I can't understand why anyone should be late for anything. Unless something disastrous happens there's no reason for it. No reason at all. I'm never late for anything…

● What impression do you get of Martyn? What do you find out about his thoughts and feelings?
● Does it sound like Martyn is speaking to you? Is his 'voice' chatty or friendly, or is it quite formal?

How does it work?

Writing in the **first person** means you only tell the story from **one point of view** – that of **the narrator**, who is the main character. As readers, we share this person's thoughts and feelings, and see everything through his or her eyes.

In the **third person** you can tell the story from **more than one viewpoint**, describing the thoughts and feelings of different characters. A third person narrator often knows everything about what is happening.

In the **first person**, careful word choice and sentence construction help create a realistic '**voice**' for your narrator. The way a person speaks or shares their thoughts can tell the reader a lot.

Now you try it

You are going to plan and write a passage in the **first person**. You are going to be writing from the viewpoint of Alex, the girl Martyn was waiting for.

1 Think about what has happened to her. Why didn't she show up? What does she think of Martyn?

2 Think about how you can create the right voice for your narrator. How would she speak? What sort of language would she use? Chatty or formal? What length or type of sentence would she use?

3 Think about how you want the reader to feel about your narrator. Do you want your reader to like the narrator, to trust her, to fear her?

4 Now draft the opening paragraph.

Development activity

Now draft the rest of your story opening. Make sure you keep your first person 'voice' going and describe only what she can see or know.

Remember

1 Stick to the voice you choose – don't swap between first and third person.

2 Create a convincing and consistent **voice** for your narrator.

Level Booster

LEVEL 4

- I can bring my writing to life
- I can choose and plan effective content
- I can choose effective verbs, nouns, adjectives and adverbs
- I can grab the reader's attention
- I can create and maintain a voice that rings true

LEVEL 5

- I can write imaginatively and thoughtfully and interest the reader
- I can plan, develop and shape my writing
- I can choose the right word, sentence, paragraph or text
- I can write vividly, powerfully, memorably
- I can develop a convincing viewpoint or role

LEVEL 6

- I can write with confidence and purpose
- I can plan apt texts for a range of purposes and audiences
- I can choose the right tone and form
- I can shape engaging and fluent texts
- I can achieve a language (word choice, style, voice, viewpoint) that suits speaker, character or purpose

Chapter 2

AF2 Produce texts which are appropriate to task, reader and purpose

This chapter is going to show you how to

- Make the purpose of your writing clear
- Use appropriate techniques in your writing
- Maintain a clear viewpoint in your writing
- Adapt information and use techniques to suit your purpose.

What's it all about?

You need to make sure the purpose of your writing is clear throughout the texts you write, and that you choose the right features and techniques to help you to do this.

This lesson will
- help you to stay focused on your purpose.

You need to think about why you are writing a particular text and make sure you make this purpose clear in what you write. You also need to choose the right level of **formality** and think about the different **writing techniques** you can use to achieve your purpose.

Getting you thinking

Imagine you have been asked to persuade a celebrity to visit your school to raise money for charity.

Read the opening paragraphs from one student's letter to David Tennant.

Dear David,

Acting in 'Dr Who' must be a tremendous experience. Every week our tutor group is gripped by your extraordinary experiences as you battle to save Earth from yet another disaster. Wouldn't it be wonderful if the special powers of the Tardis were true? We are writing to you today to offer you the chance to make a magical difference to children's lives in Thailand.

Our school is running a special fundraising fete on 24 November. Our whole school is committed to raising money for the many orphans of the 2004 Tsunami. If you were able to offer just a few hours of your valuable time, we are sure it would make a huge difference to hundreds of children's lives. Just imagine how many more visitors we would attract if we were able to say you were attending!

- How successfully do you think this student has started her letter?

How does it work?

The student uses many different techniques to try to persuade
David Tennant to visit. The letter

- starts with a **direct appeal to the reader**
- makes the **reason for writing clear** and **stays focused** on this throughout
- makes it sound as if the school will be **doing David a favour**, offering
  him the 'chance to make a magical difference'
- uses a **rhetorical question** (a question that doesn't need an answer) to
  explain how David could use the power of his celebrity to help others
- is **polite** and **formal** but also **flattering**!

Now you try it

Now read the opening from another student's letter to David Tennant.

> *Dear David,*
>
> *I am Ben in Year 9 and I am in charge of our tutor group's charity
> fundraiser at Four Green School. We are raising money for a
> children's charity in Thailand. What we're thinking is that you could
> come along to the school fete for a few hours, hopefully bringing
> your Tardis for some trips! We think that this would bring in loads
> of dosh for the school – also my mum really fancies you and would
> love to meet you! I am sure that you will want to help other people,
> David, especially as you must already have tons of money yourself...*

1 Discuss with a partner whether Ben
  - makes the main purpose of his letter clear
  - stays focused on it
  - uses any persuasive techniques
  - chooses suitably formal words.

  Find examples from the letter to support your answers.

2 Rewrite the opening of the letter to make it more persuasive.

Development activity

Write a letter to persuade a celebrity to visit your school to
raise money for charity. Think about

- what persuasive techniques you will use
- what you need to tell them about the event
- how you will make your letter sound formal.

Check your progress

LEVEL 4	I can make the main purpose of my writing clear, but don't always stay focused on it
LEVEL 5	I can make the main purpose of my writing clear and stay focused on it
LEVEL 6	I can use a range of techniques to suit my purpose and my reader

This lesson will
- help you to describe characters.

You need to be aware of the different techniques normally used in the type of text you are writing. Being a skilful writer isn't just about being able to use lots of complex techniques, but knowing *when* to use the right techniques.

Getting you thinking

In small groups, think about the **characters** that you like or find interesting in your favourite books. Together, come up with some answers to these questions:

- What makes a character – a person in a story – interesting?
- How do writers tell us about characters and make us interested in them?

How does it work?

There are lots of techniques writers use to create characters and make us interested in them. For example:

- **dialogue** (what a character says and how they speak)
- **direct description** (**adjectives** describing how a character looks; **verbs** and **adverbs** to describe how he or she moves or acts)
- **metaphors and similes** (comparing the character to something else)
- showing or telling us **how other people react to the character**
- showing or telling us **what the character thinks**
- **slowly feeding us information** about the character – to make us want to find out more.

Now you try it

Here is an extract from the novel *Raven's Gate* by Anthony Horowitz:

> Matt Freeman knew he was making a mistake.
>
> He was sitting on a low wall outside Ipswich station, wearing a grey hooded sweatshirt, shapeless, faded jeans, and trainers with frayed laces. It was six o'clock in the evening and the London train had just pulled in. Behind him, commuters were fighting their way out of the station. The concourse was a tangle of cars, taxis and pedestrians, all of them trying to find their way home. A traffic light blinked from red to green but nothing moved. Somebody leant on their horn and the noise blared out, cutting through the damp evening air. Matt heard it and looked up briefly. But the crowd meant nothing to him. He wasn't part of it. He had never been – and sometimes thought he never would be.
>
> Two men carrying umbrellas walked past and glanced at him disapprovingly. They probably thought he was up to no good. The way he was sitting – hunched forward with his knees apart – made him look somehow dangerous, and older than fourteen. He had broad shoulders, a well developed, muscular body and very bright blue, intelligent eyes. His hair was black, cut very short. Give him another five years he could be a footballer or a model – or, like plenty of others, both.
>
> His first name was Matthew but he had always called himself Matt. As the troubles had begun to pile up in his life, he had used his surname less and less until it was no longer part of him…

What techniques does the writer use to give you a sense of Matt's character? Use the list opposite to help you.

Development activity

Look at this picture. Write the opening of a story which introduces this character using the descriptive writing techniques you have explored.

Check your rogress

LEVEL 4 I can use descriptive language to describe my character

LEVEL 5 I can use describing words and some other techniques to create my character

LEVEL 6 I can use a range of writing techniques to create an interesting character

This lesson will
● help you to select and angle facts to create a viewpoint.

In some forms of writing you will need to develop and maintain a particular point of view. This means that you **select and organise** facts and details **from a certain angle**.

Getting you thinking

Look at these two articles about reducing food waste.

Food Champions

Did you know that £8 billion of food goes to waste every year? We should reduce this waste by helping people to think before they throw away food.

The Waste and Resources Action Programme has created food champions who will visit homes across the country and advise people on how to use scraps of food and turn them into tasty dishes.

This is a brilliant idea to save resources and save people money. After all, we are in the middle of a recession and every penny counts. If we can save money on food, this has to be a good idea!

Lectures on leftovers from the food police

Householders are being quizzed on their doorsteps about the amount of food they throw away.

Officials paid by a Government-backed **quango** also offer hints on recipes for leftovers.

The initiative is designed to reduce the amount of food which goes to waste – an estimated £8 billion a year.

But the officials were branded 'food police' last night and the scheme dismissed as more Government 'nannying'.

Glossary

quango: body appointed by the government

With a partner, discuss the following:
● What viewpoint does each article present?
● What information given in the first article is missing from the second article?
● What information given in the second article is missing from the first article?
● Can you find one or two words in each article which tell us what the writer thinks of the food champion scheme?

How does it work?

The articles both **select and order the facts** to present their point of view to the reader.

Each article also **chooses verbs and adjectives** carefully to present the scheme in a positive or negative light.

Now you try it

Read the article below.

Kill the Cats

Richard Evans, a member of Australia's parliament, wants all cats extinct in Australia. This is because cats that have returned to the wild are causing a big problem. There are now about 12 million feral cats in Australia and the numbers are growing.

These feral cats are responsible for killing wildlife that is very rare and only exists in Australia. Wildlife that the Australian cat preys on includes the pig-footed bandicoot, the brush-tailed bettong, the rufous hare wallaby and the Gouldian finch.

Ideas of how to get rid of cats include poisoning them, neutering them or introducing a deadly virus that will wipe them out.

It is about time Australians protected their own wildlife and got rid of the killer cat.

 Plan an article which presents the opposite viewpoint.

Development activity APP

Now write your article. Think about what **adjectives** and **verbs** you could use to describe a) cats and b) what the government is proposing to do.

Think about how you can **select and order the facts** about feral cats to persuade other people to share your viewpoint.

Remember

Select the facts and details that suit – don't include everything.

Check your progress

LEVEL 4	I can present a straightforward viewpoint in my writing
LEVEL 5	I can keep a clear viewpoint going in my writing
LEVEL 6	I can create and sustain a convincing viewpoint throughout my writing

23

This lesson will
- help you change the style of your writing to suit your purpose.

A good writer can take information from one text and use it to create another type of text. For example, you could take a piece of persuasive writing and turn it into a piece of factual writing by removing all of the persuasive devices and keeping only the facts.

To adapt what you have read, you need to have a clear understanding of **why you are writing** something. You also need to know what **techniques** are normally used in each type of writing.

Getting you thinking

Here are two texts about Brighton.

> Brighton is a seaside resort with a pier and a pleasure beach. There are over 21,000 students living in Brighton. There are many shops, cafes and places of interest in Brighton, including the Royal Pavilion. Each May, the city hosts the Brighton and Fringe festivals, the second largest Arts Festival in Britain.

Brighton's beach and famous pier and funfair have entertained generations of tourists. But there's more to Brighton than the seaside – there's the 21,000 strong student community, the labyrinth of shops and cafés in the Lanes, the elegant Royal Pavilion palace. Brighton also boasts designer outlet stores at the Marina, where you can get brand names for discount prices. Art enthusiasts can't afford to miss this year's Brighton and Fringe festivals, which will feature a line-up of international talent. Enjoy Brighton's sun and sea, but explore to enjoy its rich, cultural heart.

- What is the purpose of each text? Find evidence to support your decision.

Now you try it

Transform this factual description into a piece of persuasive writing.

- What adjectives and verbs could you use?
- How else could you persuade your reader to visit Anglesey?

Isle of Anglesey

Anglesey is separated from the mainland of north-west Wales by the Menai Strait in the Irish Sea. There are cliffs, beaches and mountains. Anglesey has one of the driest climates in Wales. There are two RSPB parks. There are 15,000 visitors every summer. Most of the coastline has been designated an Area of Outstanding Beauty. Seals, dolphins and whales have been seen in the coastal waters.

Development activity

Transform a newspaper report into a piece of creative writing.

Ambulanceman Gary Wood and decorator Colin Wright were going to see a friend when their car was buzzed by a shiny object 40ft wide.

They blacked out and swerved off the road. When they came round they carried on – only to find a 45-minute trip had taken three hours.

Under hypnosis later, both men described being abducted and medically examined by strange creatures.

The Sun (21 June 2008)

- Plan how you could adapt and develop this to make an interesting fiction story.
- Draw a spider diagram to show what you would include.
- Write your story.

Check your progress

LEVEL 4	I can make some adaptations to the information I am given to create another text
LEVEL 5	I can adapt information and use different techniques to develop a different type of writing
LEVEL 6	I can confidently adapt information and techniques to create different types of writing

Level Booster

LEVEL 4

- I can decide what type of writing I am being asked to create
- I can include the main features of that type of writing
- I can write in the correct style for a task
- I can use different techniques to interest and entertain the reader
- I can develop a clear viewpoint in my writing

LEVEL 5

- I can make the purpose of my writing clear throughout the piece
- I can include a good range of different features in a piece of writing
- I can keep the reader interested throughout a piece of writing
- I can adapt what I have read in one form and use the information in a different way in my writing

LEVEL 6

- I can be creative when writing for a range of purposes
- I can use a good range of different features to create effects
- I can sustain a viewpoint throughout a piece of writing
- I can engage the reader by writing in an interesting way
- I can adapt features from different texts to make my work more effective

Chapter 3

AF3 Organise and present whole texts effectively, sequencing and structuring information, ideas and events

This chapter is going to show you how to

- Structure your work clearly
- Build your ideas across a piece of writing
- Improve and extend your presentation skills
- Organise narrative writing effectively
- Make your ending link back to your opening.

What's it all about?

You need to organise and present texts in ways that fit your purpose for writing and appeal to your target readers. The structure of the text should make your purpose clear and hold your reader's attention.

Structure your writing clearly

This lesson will
- help you to think about the structure of your writing.

It is very important to have a structure to your writing. A clear structure helps your reader understand what you are trying to say and where your writing is going.

The way you structure your writing will depend on the purpose of the text.

Getting you thinking

- What do you think is happening in this comic strip? Write a couple of lines for each picture.
- In pairs, compare your ideas. What are the similarities and differences in the ways you have interpreted the story?

How does it work?

The writer of this comic strip put the events in a clear, **chronological** order so that the reader can easily follow what is happening. Even without words, you should be able to understand the story.

Glossary

chronological: arranged in the order in which things happened

All writers think carefully about the structure of their texts. But different structures are more appropriate for different kinds of text. For example:

- When you are writing to **inform**, you may choose to explore different aspects of the same topic in turn.
- When you are writing to **argue**, you may choose to give one point of view first and then a contrasting point of view. You might then offer your own conclusion.

Now you try it

Plan and design your own comic strip. Aim to use six frames.

Here are some ideas for your plot:

- the chase
- the argument
- the invasion

Begin by planning what each frame is going to show.

Ask yourself, 'Is it clear what is happening here?' for **every** frame you draw.

Top tips

Don't worry if you're not the best artist in the world – just try to keep it simple and neat. The most important thing is to make the structure of what is going on very clear for your reader.

Development activity

Now write a brief plan for a two minute talk on your favourite hobby, such as playing football, hockey, a musical instrument or skateboarding.

First, outline what each paragraph will be about. Make sure you have structured your ideas clearly and ordered them logically. Think about these questions:

- When did you start the hobby?
- Why did you start the hobby?
- Can you remember a particularly good or funny event?
- Has there been an incident where something went wrong?
- Why would you recommend this hobby?

Just as when you were planning your comic strip, you need to plan and organise your ideas before you start.

Top tips

Make sure all your points are made in a suitable order. Then think about how you can help your speech flow from one idea to the next. For example, 'The banjo is quite an unusual instrument. How did I decide that it was the instrument for me, I hear you ask…'

Check your progress

LEVEL 4	I can organise ideas in a logical sequence
LEVEL 5	I can organise my ideas logically and show clear links between them
LEVEL 6	I can organise my ideas to help my reader understand the overall direction of my writing

29

This lesson will
● show you how to link and build up ideas.

When you are writing, you need to stay focused on your topic and develop your ideas to build up the picture you want to create. As you write, you need to look back at what you have written and check that you are putting across your ideas effectively.

Getting you thinking

Read this extract about a trip to Death Valley, California.

> The next morning I awoke ready to see exactly how evil this unforgiving part of the globe could be. My room was cool enough with the air conditioning working full-time to cope with the heat's force. As I stepped out onto the porch in front of my room, it was as if someone had clapped their hand on my shoulder and said 'No you don't!' I took a deep breath as I headed forward, wading through the heat's powerful waves to the **sanctuary** of the breakfast room. It was still only 8 o'clock!
>
> An hour later, full of waffles and maple syrup, I headed outside once more. It was difficult to breathe as I **trudged** back through the burning heat to pack my things for the next leg of our journey. I felt like a deep-sea diver who had run out of air and was desperately trying to get to the surface […]
>
> I stopped further into the Valley and realised why it was so aptly named Death Valley. The **stifling** heat seemed to surge into the car as I opened the door, foolishly trying to plunge into its **volcanic domain**. I forced my way forward, my feet sticking to the tarmac on
> the road as everything, including me, seemed to melt. This was no place for people, or any living thing, and yet there was a group of tourists trying to inch their way towards the summit of what seemed like Everest...

Glossary

sanctuary: a place offering protection from the heat

trudged: walked wearily or slowly

stifling: so hot you can't breathe

volcanic domain: volcano-like place; in other words, it is as hot as being inside a volcano

In pairs, discuss these questions:

1 How does the text make you feel as you read it?

2 What theme (or idea) is built up throughout the piece?

3 How do you think the writer builds up this theme?

Now you try it

Write a short account of some extreme weather conditions you have experienced. It could be a very hot day by the sea, or just an intensely cold wait at a bus stop!

Think about how you could use language to describe the weather and how it affects you.

- What **nouns** and **adjectives** could you use to describe your surroundings?
- What powerful **verbs** and **adverbs** could you use to stress the effect of the weather?
- Can you use any **similes** or **metaphors** to build up the idea of the intensity of the experience?

Development activity

In groups of four, take it in turns to describe a travel experience. It could be a holiday from hell or a journey that took an unexpected turn. Spend five minutes planning and preparing your account.

Think about

- the key ideas you want to focus on
- how to structure your account so that key ideas link and build up to a climax.

Top tips

Make sure you know where your writing is going. If you don't, your reader won't either!

Check your progress		
LEVEL 4	I can organise my ideas simply using linking words and phrases	
LEVEL 5	I can develop my ideas effectively across the text	
LEVEL 6	I can structure and sequence my ideas carefully to try and influence my reader's reactions	

This lesson will
● show you how to use a range of presentational devices for effect.

It is important to present your work clearly and effectively so that a reader can easily understand what you have to say. Using different presentational techniques and devices can make a text look more attractive and encourage the reader to read on. It also signals to the reader exactly what the text is and who it is aimed at.

Remember

A text must always look right for the **audience** and **purpose**.

Getting you thinking

Look at this extract from a leaflet that is part of an Animal Aid campaign.

1 In groups of four, make a list of all the presentational devices the designer of the leaflet has used.

2 Who do you think the leaflet is aimed at?

3 What clues are there in the presentation to suggest this?

How does it work?

Many presentational devices can be used to attract the reader's interest and help the writer achieve their purpose. These include

- **pictures** – to get across a message or to attract the reader's attention
- **headings and sub-headings** – to signal what a piece of writing is about and to help the reader find information quickly
- **bullet points** – to break up and summarise information at a glance
- **font (style and size)** – to give visual interest and create a particular look
- **colour** – to attract attention and create a mood.

Now you try it

Now, in pairs, redraft and redesign a section of the Animal Aid leaflet for younger children (aged 4–7). Think about the presentational choices you could make:

- What kind of image would appeal to your target audience?
- What size and style of font would you use?
- What colours would you use?
- Are there any other features or techniques you could use?

Development activity

Now design a leaflet for pupils in your school providing helpful information on a topic. Here are some suggestions:

- How to deal with bullies
- How to keep fit and healthy
- Teenage health issues

You could use a computer to help with the layout of your leaflet. Remember to keep your audience in mind and choose presentational techniques that will help you achieve your purpose in writing.

Top tips

Use the presentational devices we have looked at in this unit. For example, you could use **bullet points** to list ideas. These help the reader pick out key points more easily.

Check your progress

LEVEL 4	I can use pictures, headings and colour to present my work effectively on the page
LEVEL 5	I can use a range of presentational features that suit the purpose and audience of my text
LEVEL 6	I can present texts imaginatively to suit my purpose and audience

This lesson will
- help you to understand and use a three part story structure.

When creating a piece of narrative writing, such as a short story or a play, you need to think about the structure of your plot. This could be a **three-part structure** with
- a **beginning** to set up the situation, introducing characters and events
- a **middle** to show the main conflict or problem
- an **end** to present the resolution of the story.

Getting you thinking

Read this extract from the novel *Tribes* by Catherine MacPhail.

> He looked around him. They were high in the building, not quite on the top floor, but near enough. Dust and broken glass lay everywhere. Behind him, the crumbling stairs he had just climbed. In front of him…
>
> Kevin gasped and stepped back. In front of him was nothing. He was standing on the edge of a gaping chasm, a hole that stretched to nothingness below. At the other side of that chasm, it looked a million miles away, was a minute stretch of floor and a smashed window. And all that connected the floor Kevin was standing on to that other side was a narrow wooden beam.
>
> Kevin looked at Torry. He was smiling, his hands on his hips. He looked at Doc. There was something **malevolent** in his eyes. And then he looked at Salom. He stepped on to the beam like an acrobat. Kevin gasped.
>
> Salom grinned. 'You get to the other side, and you are a fully paid-up member of the Tribe.'
>
> They couldn't be serious. They expected him to cross over there. Below him a sheer drop? No way!
>
> Salom stepped back and gestured to the beam, like a magician. 'Welcome,' he said, 'to the Walk of Death.'

Glossary
malevolent: evil, nasty

- In pairs, decide what is happening in the story.
- What part of the story do you think this section is taken from?

Now you try it

Read the following extracts from the middle of two stories.

Decide which one works best and why.

1

Detective Inspector Eames yawned. The murder enquiry was going nowhere. There were three suspects. Any one of them could have murdered Sean Nash.

Eames looked at his file again. Nothing! He needed a break, he needed something to happen.

2

The gun men were closing in. Martin bit his lip. He knew the killers were not far away. It was either face the killers or jump from one cliff edge to another. Hobson's choice really. Martin decided to jump.

He took a deep breath and ran fast, faster, faster. He must jump at his best. He could feel his heart beating in his chest. Thump, thump, thump. Like a drum.

He couldn't hesitate now. Hesitation, fear… they were his enemies.

Development activity APP

Plan the three-part plot of an exciting action story and write from the middle. Remember to keep it interesting and exciting – don't let the middle sag.

Now allow your partner to read the middle. See if your partner can guess what might happen at the start of the story.

Write a start and end to your story. When finished, you should have a great story!

Remember

It is very important to plan first, so that you know where your story is going. Use paragraphs to help structure and organise your ideas.

Check your progress

LEVEL 4	I can organise simple stories with fitting openings and endings
LEVEL 5	I can use the three-part narrative structure to organise my writing
LEVEL 6	I can use and adapt the three-part narrative structure to organise my writing effectively

This lesson will
- show you how to link your conclusion to your opening
- show you how to set out a formal letter.

It is important to link your conclusion back to your introduction. This is particularly important when writing arguments and persuasive texts because you want to remind your reader of your purpose for writing, and return to the key points you made in your introduction.

Getting you thinking

In pairs, read this piece of persuasive writing.

Would you really like to be a Victorian child?

A lot of people think the past was something wonderful: the good old days, when things were better. Well, think again!

If you were lucky enough to stay at home you would probably have had to care for your younger brothers and sisters. Children as young as four or five were left in the house to look after their siblings while their parents worked.

Some boys were made to work as chimney sweeps. They were chosen because they were agile as well as small. These boys had to work in hot, dark cramped conditions. Most boys scraped their legs, elbows and knees as they climbed up inside the chimney. They had to have their flesh hardened by rubbing it with salt water. If they failed to do this properly, they were caned.

If anyone became stuck in the narrow chimney space, the sweep made a fire, to smoke the boy down.

Those who went to school fared little better. Teachers regularly used the cane. Some teachers chose thin canes because they hurt more. The teacher would hit pupils hard and the slender cane would rebound and hit the pupil again. So if the teacher hit a boy once, the boy got two strokes!

For badly behaved children, there was no place like remove. Instead, naughty pupils were put in the stocks and left there. Some schools had a basket called the cage. Pupils were put in the cage and it was raised by rope until it almost reached the classroom ceiling. The class continued with the pupil left in the cage.

So you'd really like to be a Victorian, would you? Personally, I'd rather be growing up in the 21st Century.

- What do you notice about the opening and the ending of the article?

How does it work?

The opening usually tells the reader what the article is about.

The middle part expands on the opening, making **points that are relevant to the purpose** and that flow in a logical order.

The **conclusion** should always link back to the point made in the introduction. The final paragraph should remind the reader of what the writer is trying to say.

Now you try it

Write a letter to your school newspaper persuading your school to take action on an issue you care about.

Think about
- how you will introduce the topic
- how you will make your letter persuasive
- keeping the focus on the subject you are writing about
- linking back to your original point in the conclusion.

Your issue can relate to school or the world outside. Try to write four or five paragraphs.

Remember to
- Put your address in the top right-hand corner.
- Put the date underneath it.
- Begin with 'Dear ...'
- End with 'Yours sincerely' when writing to someone you know by name and 'Yours faithfully' when you have used 'Dear Sir/Madam' at the start.

Top tips

Letters often end with a 'call to action', telling the reader what the writer wants them to do.

Development activity

Use your IT skills to redraft your letter. Then, in groups of four, put your letters together, to make a letters page for classroom display.

Check your progress

LEVEL 4	I can write a clear introduction and conclusion, which may be linked
LEVEL 5	I can write an effective conclusion that refers back to my introduction
LEVEL 6	I can write an introduction that signals the direction of my text and an effective conclusion

Level Booster

LEVEL 4

- I can organise my writing
- I can write an effective opening
- I can use linking words and devices appropriately
- I can keep my writing organised
- I can write an appropriate conclusion

LEVEL 5

- I can structure my work clearly
- I can develop my material across the whole piece of writing
- I can develop clear links between my paragraphs
- I can make my ending link back to the opening
- I can organise my sentences into proper paragraphs

LEVEL 6

- I can skilfully control the organisation of my writing
- I can write with a specific reader in mind
- I can use opening paragraphs to introduce themes clearly
- I can use linking devices between paragraphs
- I can anticipate what the readers' questions may be

Chapter 4

AF4 Construct paragraphs and use cohesion within and between paragraphs

This chapter is going to show you how to

- Use paragraphs in fiction
- Link ideas within and between paragraphs
- Use paragraphs in non-fiction texts
- Sequence paragraphs to give information effectively
- Organise poems using stanzas.

What's it all about?

Using paragraphs to make the ideas in your writing clear and create helpful links for your reader

1 Use paragraphs in fiction

This lesson will
- show you how to begin a new paragraph in a story.

When writing fiction, such as a novel or short story, writers use paragraphs to help the reader follow the events.

Getting you thinking

Read this extract from the novel *Thursday's Child* by Sonya Hartnett. Harper's brother Tin has been caught in a mudslide and Harper is discussing this with her father.

'I didn't mean to let Tin get caught in a mudslide. I told him not to go near the water, I told him it wasn't safe. It was just an accident, Da. Audrey twisted my ear.'

'Hurt?'

I nodded sombrely. Da wiped his hair from his eyes.

'She was wrong to do that to your ear. Nobody can do anything about mud. It's one of those things that has a will of its own.'

I knew he was remembering being a soldier: Da said that in the war a whole country had changed into mud. The muddy country had **suctioned** down entire bodies of men and horses and no one saw a hair of them again. Da said that the soldiers would dig and dig frantically, **spurred on** by **gargling** screams, but the mud had a teasing nature and would suck its captive deeper just as the shovels were finding him, just as hands were reaching to clasp.

Glossary

suctioned: sucked

spurred on: urged on

gargling: choking with liquid mud (gargling means to rinse your throat with liquid)

- With a partner, decide why the writer has started each new paragraph in this extract.

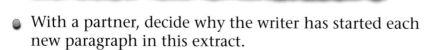

How does it work?

There are several different reasons for starting a new paragraph in a story.

It can show

- a change of **speaker**
- a change of **place** (this could be a small shift in place such as a person having walked into a house, or a huge shift in place such as the action switching to an astronaut on the moon)
- a change of **time** (when the action shifts forwards or backwards in time – this could be as little as a minute or thousands of years!)
- a change of **topic**.

Now you try it

Read this extract from the same novel and decide where the paragraph breaks should go.

> From my place lying on the floor before the fire, I did not need to look up to know Da's eyes had darted to me. 'It was Tin, Mam,' I said listlessly. 'Ah,' Da exclaimed, and his hand slapped the table. 'What do you mean it was Tin?' 'Harper, enough!' I crooked my neck to peer at him. 'We have to tell, Da. People are asking.'

Development activity

Now write your own one-page short story. Remember to start a new paragraph whenever there is a change of speaker, place or time.

Your story could be about a granddad. He is comforting his grandchild who has fallen over and is hurt. He might reflect on his own childhood, when he was hurt in a farming accident.

Or a war hero might watch his grandchildren play a war game. He might tell them about his real war experience.

Check your progress

LEVEL 4	I can start a new paragraph whenever dialogue is used
LEVEL 5	I can start new paragraphs when the action shifts
LEVEL 6	I can use new paragraphs when there is a change of speaker, place and time

This lesson will
- show you how to link paragraphs.

It is important to link sentences in your paragraphs and to create links between paragraphs. It helps your reader understand how your ideas connect and develop.

Getting you thinking

Read the opening of this short story.

> Old Jack Morpeth knew there was something dangerous in the cellar.
>
> He also knew he had to keep the terrible secret to himself. He had kept the secret for years.
>
> One evening, Jack's nephew came to visit. He wanted to play a game of chess. Halfway through the game, they could both hear a horrible noise coming from the cellar.
>
> Jack knew he could no longer keep his terrible secret to himself.

- With a partner, discuss how the writer creates links between the sentences and connections between the paragraphs.

How does it work?

The writer links the sentences within each paragraph by building from the initial idea that there is something dangerous in the cellar.

To create links, the writer uses

- **pronouns** such as 'he' to refer back to characters who have already been named.
- **synonyms** to add further details to the initial idea: 'dangerous', 'terrible', 'horrible'.
- **time connectives**, such as 'One evening', to link one paragraph to the next.
- **repeated words and phrases**. In the final paragraph, the 'terrible secret' is mentioned again. This refers back to the first paragraph, only now we know it won't be a secret for much longer…

Glossary

pronouns: words such as he, she, it, they, we, I and you

synonyms: words with the same meaning

Now you try it

Look at these ideas for a short story about a boy who achieves his dream of travelling by hot air balloon.

Steven went hot air ballooning for a birthday treat.

Steven had always wanted to have a ride in a hot air balloon.

Steven used to dream about climbing into the basket and looking up at the sky.

When Steven stepped into the basket there was this really loud noise – the noise of the burners.

When Steven left the ground he felt really cold.

When the balloon reached the top of the trees, Steven looked down and saw people below who looked as small as ants.

Steven could see the ground laid out like a patchwork blanket, just like he had imagined it in his dream.

Using the linking techniques you have explored, draft the short story, imagining what happened next. Remember to

- use paragraphs to organise your writing
- use pronouns to refer back to nouns you have used already
- use synonyms to link ideas
- use time connectives such as 'Then', 'Until' and 'After' to link paragraphs and order events.

Development activity

Short summaries on the back cover of books are called blurbs. Blurbs are designed to attract readers and should be written in short, punchy paragraphs. With a partner take a look at the blurb of one of your favourite books and identify the different techniques the writer uses to link sentences and paragraphs.

Now write your own three-paragraph blurb about a book you have read. It should tell the reader:

- what sort of book it is
- a brief idea of the plot – without giving too much away
- how much someone will enjoy it.

Remember

Use the techniques you have explored to link the sentences and paragraphs in your blurb.

Check your progress

LEVEL 4 I can recognise connections between paragraphs

LEVEL 5 I can recognise and use connections between paragraphs

LEVEL 6 I can link sentences in my paragraphs and create links between paragraphs

43

This lesson will
● show you how to order paragraphs in an interesting way.

Paragraphs need to be ordered in a clear and logical way when you write non-fiction texts. You can use a variety of approaches to do this, depending on the type of text you are writing.

Getting you thinking

With a partner, read this essay which explores the arguments for and against the idea of setting a curfew for teenagers under 17.

Should there be a curfew on teenagers below the age of 17?

In modern Britain, we experience all sorts of crime. Many people believe that it is possible to cut down on crime. It has been suggested that any teenager from the age of 13 to 16 should not be allowed out of their homes after 9.30pm until 7am the next morning – unless they are with a parent or guardian.

An argument for this idea is that teenagers are very likely to be involved in crimes such as car theft, car vandalism, general vandalism and low-level nuisance, such as knock and run. Most of this sort of crime takes place at night. If teenagers were made to stay at home, these crimes would end.

However, the proposal would stop teenagers from joining safe and organised activities and events. It would also stop some law-abiding teenagers from doing their newspaper or milk rounds early in the morning.

Equally, though, in parts of the USA crime has been reduced by introducing curfews for teenagers. There are parts of Britain where teenage crime and nuisance is a problem, so something has to be done about it! There needs to be a curfew, but it might be better to impose it on children aged 10 to 14. After the age of 14, teenagers should be responsible for their own actions. Also, teenage crime isn't a problem in every part of the country. Perhaps local councils should have a curfew system that they think will work in their area.

● Identify the main point made in each paragraph.
● Label each paragraph as either **for** or **against** the argument.
● Discuss what the writer's conclusion is.

How does it work?

- The first paragraph is the **introduction**. It tells the reader what the essay will be about.
- The second paragraph sets out the arguments **for the proposal**. It develops the first by stating: 'An argument for this idea is…'.
- The third paragraph changes viewpoint by setting out the arguments **against the proposal**. It links to the second by using the connective, 'However…'.
- Paragraph four **concludes** the piece. It uses another connective, 'Equally', to draw the two viewpoints together and to introduce the writer's own concluding viewpoint.

Now you try it

1 Think about the proposal: the driving age should be lowered to 14.

2 With a partner, jot down the ideas you could include in an argumentative essay on this subject.

3 Now, on your own, plan your essay paragraph by paragraph. Think about what information will go where and why, as well as when to use a new paragraph. You may wish to switch between different points of view, for example. Conclude with your own viewpoint.

Development activity

Compare your essay plan with a partner's. Discuss how you could use some of these connectives to link your paragraphs:

However	Similarly	Alternatively	More importantly	Equally
In the same way	In contrast	On the other hand	On one hand	Secondly
In the first place	To conclude	Nevertheless	Moreover	First

4 Sequence paragraphs to give information effectively

This lesson will
- show you how to write information sheets using paragraphs.

Some writing is meant to **inform**, so that the reader ends up knowing more about a subject. In this type of writing, paragraphs need to be set out logically in order to lead you through a process or to present facts in a way that is easy to understand.

Getting you thinking

Read this advice sheet about snowboarding.

Snowboarding can be a dangerous sport. It is not a good idea to be launched down a slope by some well meaning but reckless friend who cheerfully shouts out instructions as you lurch dangerously near a cliff edge. It is much better to have proper lessons from a qualified snowboard instructor.

With a qualified instructor at a recognised snowboard school, you will learn how to snowboard faster and more safely. You will be taught techniques such as the really important skill of stopping by using the board. Much better than smashing into a pine tree!

Some people are frightened about starting lessons. Why are people frightened? As in everything else, we're scared of the unknown. We allow our imaginations to take over. We don't know what being on a snowboard feels like. We wonder what will happen if we make mistakes. That's why we all need qualified instructors.

Snowboarding is most certainly a sideways sport. When snowboarders move down a slope, they lead with one foot. Left footers are known as regular or natural riders and right footers are called Goofies. Goofy, the Disney character, surfed right footed! You will quickly learn which foot is your lead foot.

So, why not book a lesson and find out? It's fun!

- With a partner, create a flow-chart showing the main point made in each paragraph.

How does it work?

The advice sheet is ordered by topic. Each paragraph is linked to the one before it.

Now you try it

In pairs, re-read the advice sheet opposite about snowboarding.

- Do you think this advice sheet is written well?
- Do you think the writer has missed out any important information – if so, what?
- Look at the first paragraph – is it too long, too short or just right? Give reasons for your answer.
- The information is in five paragraphs. To produce a more flowing piece of writing, could any of the paragraphs be combined? If so, which ones?

Development activity

1 Think of a subject you know well.

2 Find out more information about it by using the library or researching on the internet.

3 Now bullet-point your ideas or use a spider diagram to plan an advice sheet for teenagers about your chosen subject.

For example, if you had chosen to write about swimming, you could plan like this:

- Introduction to swimming
- How to swim the breaststroke
- How to swim the crawl
- The dos and don'ts of swimming
- Life-saving techniques

Think about the order of your paragraphs and then draft your advice sheet.

Check your progress

LEVEL 4 I can use paragraphs to present facts

LEVEL 5 I can present facts in a way that is easy to understand

LEVEL 6 I can present ordered paragraphs and I can redraft

This lesson will
- show you how to organise poems into stanzas.

Poetry has different rules from fiction. Instead of paragraphs, poems use sets of lines. These are called stanzas.

Getting you thinking

Read this poem by Steve Turner.

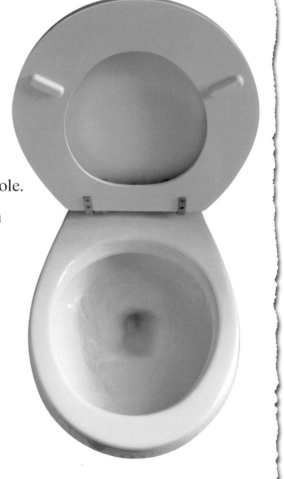

The Day I Fell Down the Toilet

The day I fell down the toilet
Is a day I'll never forget,
One moment I was in comfort
The next I was helpless and wet.

My feet tipped up to the ceiling
My body collapsed in the bowl,
In haste I grabbed at the handle
And found myself flushed down a hole.

One wave goodbye to the bathroom
And I was lost in the sewer,
Travelling tunnels and caverns
On a raft made out of manure.

Then came the washing-up water
With bits of spaghetti and peas,
The filth from the local factory
And an undiscovered disease.

Drifting along in the darkness,
There was nothing to do but wait.
What would I say to my mum now?
What was it that made me so late?

- With a partner, write a sentence for each stanza explaining what it is about.

How does it work?

Each stanza is about a new topic.

The stanzas have a regular rhythm and rhyme scheme. In each stanza the second and fourth lines rhyme, and every line of the poem has eight syllables. This gives the poem a bouncy, regular pace and helps to create a humorous mood.

Other poems might not tell a story, but describe a place or an emotion. These poems might change stanza to show a change of place, time or viewpoint in a similar way to how paragraphs are used in stories.

Now you try it

The last stanza is missing. How will the poem end? Remember, it should link to stanza five but also introduce a new idea.

- Think about how you can maintain the rhyme scheme and rhythm. You could also think up a list of rhyming words to include.
- Write a four-line stanza to end the poem using the same rhyme scheme and number of syllables per line.

Development activity

Turn this *unformed* text into a poem of your own.

- Decide how many stanzas you will use, and explain to a partner why you have started each new stanza.
- Choose where you will break each line, again explaining why you have made this decision.

the mobile stops ringing the girl starts crying big tears like pearls drop the train passengers look away embarrassed when the train gets to the station everyone leaves not the girl she stares at the rain outside somewhere on the platform an MP3 is playing someone is singing a sad song for lovers in another town a boy dries his own tears turns up the radio turns off his mobile

Remember

There is no right or wrong answer but think hard about *why* you are organising it in this way.

Level Booster

LEVEL 4

- I can support my main point with other sentences
- I can link ideas between paragraphs
- I can begin to vary sentences within a paragraph
- I can recognise the use of stanzas in poetry

LEVEL 5

- I can use paragraphs to signal a change of subject, speaker, time or place
- I can sequence paragraphs in a logical way
- I can order paragraphs by topic or viewpoint
- I can make logical links between paragraphs
- I can recognise and write poetry using stanzas

LEVEL 6

- I can shape paragraphs quickly and coherently
- I can order paragraphs logically and effectively
- I can order paragraphs in fiction and non-fiction by theme
- I can create varied and clear bridges between paragraphs
- I can write poetry using interesting stanzas

Chapter 5

AF5 Vary sentences for clarity, purpose and effect

This chapter is going to show you how to

- Turn simple sentences into complex sentences
- Use subordinate clauses
- Vary your sentence lengths and structures
- Use connectives and vary the order of clauses
- Use different tenses for effect.

What's it all about?

Using varied sentence structures with confidence will make your sentences interesting to read and improve your writing.

This lesson will
- show you how to use complex sentences in your writing.

Getting you thinking

Look at the following passage:

> The man looked suspicious. He walked with a ladder. He put it against a window. Then he climbed up the ladder. Then he opened the window. Then he tried to climb through the window and got inside.

- Does this read like your writing?

How does it work?

The sentences above all sound the same. The whole passage could be improved by using some **complex sentences** to add detail and variety.

Look at the following words. They are called **connectives**.

after	although	because	before	if
so	since	though	how	until
when	while	where	wherever	as

These words are often used when you add information to a **simple** sentence to turn it into a **complex** sentence.

For example, the first sentence in the passage above could be rewritten with more detail to become this:

Although the man looked suspicious, nobody stopped him.

When these words begin the sentence, a comma should be placed after the first part of the sentence.

Although I had a heavy cold, I still ran the race.

Until I do my work, my mum will force me to stay inside.

While I watch the match, Collette will be with her friends.

Now you try it

Complete the sentences below to create four complex sentences.

1 Although it was raining, …
2 When I was younger, …
3 Because he was bad tempered, …
4 Unless we can think of a plan, …

Development activity

You can also make your sentences more interesting by experimenting with the word order.

The extra information you add to make a complex sentence can come at the **start**, **middle** or **end** of the sentence.

We are doomed unless we can think of a plan.
Unless we can think of a plan, we are doomed.
We are, unless we can think of a plan, doomed.

Notice where the commas are placed in each example.

1 Look at the following sentences and try to change the word order of each in at least one way.

  a Until the last moment, I thought Blackburn would win.
  b When the going gets tough, the tough get going.
  c Before I met you, life was dull.

2 Look back at the passage on the previous page. How could you make it more exciting? Rewrite the passage by

  ○ adding **detail**
  ○ turning **simple** sentences into **complex** sentences
  ○ trying out **different word orders** in your sentences
  ○ imagining what happens next.

Check your progress

LEVEL 4	I can use some variety of sentence structure
LEVEL 5	I can vary my sentence structures with complex sentences
LEVEL 6	I can effectively control my use of complex sentences

This lesson will
- introduce you to main and subordinate clauses
- show you how to use clauses with who / whom, that / which, and whose.

A complex sentence will contain a **main clause** and one or more **subordinate clauses**.

Getting you thinking

A **clause** is a group of words that contains
- a subject (someone or something that is doing or being something)
- a predicate (the other words in a clause. This must always include a verb.)

Example:

Volunteers collected the litter after a festival.
(subject) (verb) (predicate)

Simple sentences contain only one clause.

Compound sentences are made up of two or more clauses of equal strength, joined by **coordinating conjunctions** (and, or, but, yet).

Example:

The twins camped out at the festival **and** enjoyed every minute.
(clause one) (conjunction) (clause two)

How does it work?

Sometimes one clause is weaker than the other. The weaker one is called a **subordinate clause**. The stronger one is called the **main clause**. Together, the clauses make a **complex sentence**.

The Hot Potato group, which had flown in by helicopter, was the best act.

main clause   subordinate clause   main clause

The **subordinate clause** usually just adds information to the main clause. The main clause would still work without the subordinate clause.

The Hot Potato group was the best act.

Subordinate clauses which give us more information about people or things are introduced by words such as **who**, **whom**, **that**, **which** and **whose**.

Now you try it

The following sentences are missing their subordinate clauses. Add the correct subordinate clause to the sentences below. You will also need to add commas, as in the example.

Example:

My brother often got into trouble at school.

My brother, who was very talkative, often got into trouble at school.

Simple sentences:

1 Our puppy chews almost everything.
2 Amanda Higgins always gets her homework done.
3 The overweight horse is not a champion.

Subordinate clauses:

whose mother is a teacher

who is very playful

which ate the hay

Development activity

Write a short, informative paragraph about your favourite pop star or band. Make sure you include some sentences with subordinate clauses, using **who / whom**, **which / that**, or **whose**.

Check your progress

LEVEL 4	I understand subordinate clauses
LEVEL 5	I can understand and use subordinate clauses
LEVEL 6	I can write using a variety of subordinate clauses

55

This lesson will
● help you to think about sentence length and structure.

A **long** sentence can build up tension and drama.
A **short** one can deliver a shock or surprise.

Getting you thinking

In *Great Expectations* by Charles Dickens, Pip, a lonely young orphan, visits his parents' and brothers' graves in a churchyard in the Kentish marshes.

> At such a time I found out for certain, that this bleak place overgrown with nettles was the churchyard; and that Philip Pirrip, late of this parish, and also Georgiana wife of the above, were dead and buried; and that Alexander, Bartholomew, Abraham, Tobias, and Roger, infant children of the **aforesaid**, were also dead and buried; and that the dark flat wilderness beyond the churchyard, **intersected** with dykes and mounds and gates, with scattered cattle feeding on it, was the marshes; and that the low leaden line beyond, was the river; and that the distant savage lair from which the wind was rushing, was the sea; and that the small bundle of shivers growing afraid of it all and beginning to cry, was Pip.
>
> 'Hold your noise!' cried a terrible voice, as a man started up from among the graves at the side of the church porch. 'Keep still, you little devil, or I'll cut your throat!'

Glossary

aforesaid: the two parent mentioned before

intersected: cut across

● With a partner, discuss the different types of sentence Dickens uses in this extract and what effect they have on you as a reader.

Now you try it

Charles Dickens also wrote a short story called *The Haunted House*. Here is his first description of this creepy place.

It was a **solitary** house, standing in a neglected garden. It was uninhabited, but had, within a year or two, been cheaply repaired to make it **habitable**; I say cheaply, because the work had been done in a surface manner, and was already decaying as to the paint and plaster. A lop-sided board drooped over the garden wall, announcing that it was 'to let on very reasonable terms, well furnished'. It was much too closely and heavily shadowed by trees, and, in particular, there were six tall poplars before the front windows, which were excessively **melancholy**. It was easy to see that it was an avoided house – a house that nobody would take. And the natural **inference** was that it had the reputation of being a haunted house…

Imagine that you explore this house. You find something shocking in an upstairs room.

- Use **long sentences** to describe crossing the garden, pushing open the front door, exploring the downstairs rooms, climbing the stairs and then forcing open a locked bedroom.
- Use **very short sentences** to reveal what is in the mysterious room.

Glossary

solitary: lonely or by itself

habitable: suitable to live in

melancholy: sad or depressing

inference: conclusion

Development activity

Compare your description with a partner's. Ask your partner for feedback. Then redraft your description.

Check your progress		
LEVEL 4	I can try to vary the length and structure of sentences	
LEVEL 5	I can vary my sentences to give them force and clarity	
LEVEL 6	I can control varied sentences for effect	

This lesson will
- help you to link and vary the order of your sentences.

If you can link and order your sentences well, it will make your writing clearer and help you to stress the most important points.

How does it work?

Connectives are useful to link separate sentences, especially in formal writing like reports, letters or arguments.

The following words and phrases are particularly useful:

so	by contrast	similarly	next	however	finally
thus	therefore	for example	above all	consequently	in conclusion

For example:

- No answer has been received. **Consequently**, this country is at war.
- Some marriages end in divorce. Many, **however**, are happy and long-lasting.

Connectives can be used at the **start**, in the **middle** or at the **end** of a sentence.

Word order. Try to experiment with the order of your sentences to make them more forceful or to help you stress particular information.

Look at this sentence:

> I am sending you to prison for twenty years, despite your previous good record and difficult family life.

The order could be changed to focus the reader's attention on the fact the person is being sent to prison:

> Despite your previous good record and difficult family life, I am sending you to prison for twenty years.

Now you try it

1 Relate these pairs of sentences, using a connective from the table opposite.

- I am quite tall. My brother is surprisingly short.
- This film is exciting, and has memorable characters and amazing settings. It is totally brilliant.
- The evidence is overwhelming. I find you guilty of this awful crime.

2 Now experiment with the order of these sentences. Discuss with a partner the effects of your changes.

- Out there in the wilderness, the children were waiting.
- Without your support and generous donations, the High Cross Animal Centre could not survive.

Development activity

Look at this information sheet about J K Rowling.

Joanne Rowling was twenty-five when she first thought up Harry Potter.

The idea came on a train from Manchester to London in 1990.

She had no pen and paper at hand. She invented the school of wizards and Harry in her head.

She set down the first notes in a cheap notebook.

She made many other jottings which soon filled a shoe-box.

She planned seven books about Harry from the first, one for each of his school years.

Some of the first book was written in an Edinburgh café.

She earned a living from secretarial work while she prepared the first book in detail.

She sent an outline and three specimen chapters to the Christopher Little Literary Agency.

Bryony Evens, an editorial assistant at Little's, spotted the magic of the book.

Several publishers refused *Harry Potter*. It was published by Bloomsbury in 1997.

J K Rowling has become world famous. She has made many millions of pounds from the *Harry Potter* books.

Use the techniques you have learned to help you to write a short and exciting biography of the author of *Harry Potter*.

You can use any of the information on the sheet above.

Look at these websites to find some extra details:

http://www.bloomsbury.com/Authors/details.aspx?tpid=720

http://www.bloomsbury.com/HarryPotter/

Remember

Use connectives to link sentences together.

Experiment with the order of your sentences to stress the key information and start sentences in different ways.

Check your progress

LEVEL 4	I can write correct simple and compound sentences
LEVEL 5	I can use connectives to vary the order of my sentences
LEVEL 6	I can vary the order of my sentences for effect

59

This lesson will

● tell you more about the **tenses and forms of verbs** and show you how to use them in your writing.

Verbs are the words that tell us about

● **actions** (hit, run, cook, walk, lift). Most verbs are **doing words**.

● **states of being** (seem, am).

How does it work?

Tense shows us the time of the verb (**past**, **present** or **future**).

I saw	I see	I shall/will see
past	**present**	**future**

Some tenses are **continuous**. The action or state goes on for some time.

I was eating	I am eating	I shall/will be eating
past	**present**	**future**

Continuous tenses are formed with **present participles**.

Participles are parts of verbs.

● A **present participle** ends in -ing: going

You must add an **auxiliary verb** to a **present participle** to make it into a complete verb:

I am going to the cinema on Friday.
auxiliary + participle = complete verb

It is the same with the **past continuous**.

I was going to visit my granny.
auxiliary + participle = complete verb

Remember

There is one classic mistake connected with th[e] verb 'do':

I **done** my homework a[t] school.

Many people say or even write this but it is the wron[g] form. 'Did' is the past tens[e] of 'do'.

I **did** my homework at school.

Now you try it

1 The present tense can be very effective in story writing. It adds excitement by suggesting that events are taking place before our eyes.

You are writing a story set in Victorian times about the mysterious Lady Audley, who has a strange secret in her life. The narrator of your story meets her at night in the large garden of the great country house where she lives with her rich husband. The narrator wants to discover her secret.

In your first draft, you use the past tense.

> Brilliant moonlight allowed me to find the tree-shaded lime walk where we had arranged to meet. My feet rustled the fallen leaves. A dog was barking nervously. An owl shrieked. Across the frosty lawn, a dark figure, wrapped in a cloak, advanced to meet me. I could see her frosty breath in the cold air. I whispered a greeting. Would she finally tell me about her mysterious secret?

You decide this would be even better in the present tense. Rewrite the passage, changing all the verbs from past to present.

2 Sport really comes alive in the present tense. We like to see or hear what is happening in the match **NOW**!

Here is a football commentary in the past tense. Recast it into the present tense to make it come alive.

> Smith flicked the ball across the goal mouth. Jones, the defender, completely missed it. Rogers raced across and back-heeled the ball to Brown. A neat header sent the ball into the back of the net. It was a GOAL!

Development activity

Robert Southey, a nineteenth century poet, wrote a poem for his children about the waterfalls of Lodore in the Lake District. He did it all with present participles!

> Retreating and beating and meeting and sheeting,
> Delaying and straying and playing and spraying,
> Advancing and prancing and glancing and dancing,
> Recoiling, turmoiling and toiling and boiling,
> And rushing and flushing and brushing and gushing…

Write a description of pupils leaving school when the afternoon bell rings, using as many participles as you can. Divide them with 'and' or commas.

Check your progress

LEVEL 4	I can get most verb forms and tenses right	
LEVEL 5	I can use verb forms and tenses correctly and effectively in more complicated sentences	
LEVEL 6	I can use verb forms and tenses for strong effect in varied sentence patterns	

Level Booster

LEVEL 4

- I can write and check simple and compound sentences
- I can write more complicated sentences with conjunctions
- I can try out complex sentences

LEVEL 5

- I can understand main and subordinate clauses
- I can use various kinds of subordinate clause
- I can think about sentence length, structure and word order
- I can use connectives to link and relate ideas
- I can understand and use different tenses of verbs

LEVEL 6

- I can vary my sentence patterns for emphasis and effect
- I can use simple, compound and complex sentences to suit my purpose

AF6 Write with technical accuracy of syntax and punctuation in phrases, clauses and sentences

This chapter is going to show you how to

- Use speech punctuation effectively
- Use apostrophes in informal writing
- Use apostrophes for possession
- Use semicolons accurately
- Use colons accurately.

What's it all about?

Using speech marks, apostrophes, colons and semicolons accurately to improve your writing.

Use speech punctuation effectively

This lesson will
- help you to use correct punctuation and layout of written speech.

It is important to present speech accurately and to use the correct punctuation, so that your reader can follow your text.

Getting you thinking

Revise what you know about the layout and punctuation of conversation. With a partner, read this dialogue between two characters.

'I love reading ghost stories,' said Dan.

comma goes inside speech marks

'Do you believe in ghosts?' asked Debbie.

question mark goes inside speech marks

full stop at the end of the first sentence

'I don't believe in them,' Dan replied. 'I just like the excitement of haunted houses and spooky happenings.'

'I prefer books about real life problems!' Debbie exclaimed.

'You read what you like,' laughed Dan, 'and I'll stick to ghosts and horrors.'

comma because spoken sentence is broken

second line of speech returns to margin

How does it work?

You need to remember that speech marks go round the actual words of a speaker. Also

- Use single speech marks.
- Each new speaker starts a new paragraph.
- Indent each new speaker 2 cm (handwriting) or one tab (computer) from the margin.
- Any punctuation in the speech itself goes inside the speech marks.
- We often break off our sentences in speech. Such a break is marked by an ellipsis (…) or a dash (–).

Now you try it

Add punctuation to the rest of Debbie's and Dan's conversation:

> Well I did once see a good ghost story on television said Debbie It was about a haunted railway in Victorian times It really scared me
>
> Oh yes answered Dan I've seen that too The ghost is very frightening It warns people about horrible railway accidents on that stretch of line

Development activity

Written speech can be a very dramatic way to tell a story.

In Charles Dickens' story *The Signalman*, the narrator talks to a lonely signalman working on an isolated stretch of railway. He has seen a hooded figure waving and shouting by the mouth of a tunnel.

○ With a partner, read their conversation and look at the punctuation and layout used. Do you notice anything unusual?

'Who is it?'

'I don't know. I never saw the face. The left arm is across the face and the right arm is waved – violently waved. This way.'

I followed his action with my eyes…

'One moonlight night,' said the man, 'I was sitting here when I heard a voice cry "Halloa! Below there!" I started up, looked from that door, and saw this someone else standing by the red light near the tunnel, waving as I just now showed you. The voice seemed hoarse with shouting, and it cried, "Look out! Look out!" I caught up my lamp, turned it on red, and ran towards the figure calling, "What's wrong? What has happened? Where?" I wondered at its keeping the sleeve across its eyes. I ran right up at it, and had my hand stretched out to pull the sleeve away, when it was gone.'

A terrible rail crash in the tunnel happens soon afterwards. The ghost appears a second time at dawn six months later. This time it is silent and covers its face with both hands.

○ Following the rules of speech punctuation, write the conversation between the narrator and the signalman who saw the ghost, explaining what happened.

Top tips

For speech within speech, or for a quotation within a quotation, use double speech marks.

Check your progress

LEVEL 4	I can use some speech punctuation
LEVEL 5	I can write and punctuate written speech
LEVEL 6	I can use speech punctuation accurately

2 Use apostrophes in informal writing

This lesson will
● help you to use apostrophes to create an informal tone.

Contractions are often used in **informal writing**, especially in speech. It is important to know how to write them correctly.

Getting you thinking

Contractions are short forms of words where one or more letters have been missed out. They are very common in dialogue because we tend to run words together when we speak.

You can also use contractions in non-fiction writing to create an informal tone, though you should avoid them in more formal writing like reports, application letters and essays.

With a partner, decide how you would write the contraction in each of these phrases:

are not   he would   it is   we will   they have

Remember to think about which letters will be missing!

How does it work?

A common mistake is to put the apostrophe between the original words, for example: are'nt.

The rule is simple: to make a contraction, put the apostrophe in place of the missing letter or letters:

aren't   he'd   it's   we'll   they've

Beware, though – not all contractions follow this rule:
● 'will not' changes to 'won't'
● 'shall not' changes to 'shan't'
● 'cannot' changes to 'can't'

You also see apostrophes for contraction in **archaic (outdated) language** in poems and plays:

'twas (it was)   o'er (over)   'tis (it is)

You still need them in **old forms** that we have kept:

o'clock (of the clock)

You do not need apostrophes in contractions that have made themselves into **new words**:
● bus   (used to be <u>omnibus</u>)
● phone   (can still be <u>telephone</u>)
● flu   (can still be <u>influenza</u>)

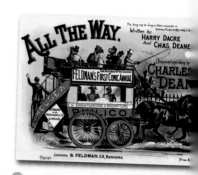

Now you try it

Using contractions, rewrite this email from the organisers of a music festival. Try to make the email sound more informal.

> I am afraid the Cool Vibes Festival is sold out. We did not expect to have so much interest in tickets. We would have called you directly to confirm that your booking had been unsuccessful, but we cannot find a record of your telephone number. I will put your name on the reserve list for tickets in case we have any returns. You are welcome to contact me if you have any queries.

Development activity

Three teenagers, Pete, Lyndsay and Kamal, are the sole survivors of a shipwreck on a desert island in the Pacific. They sit on the beach, checking their resources and making plans.

They have these things:

shorts	a mobile phone but no charger!
rucksacks	a lighter (half-empty)
no food	one bottle of water
T-shirts	flip flops

The island has these features:

beautiful white sandy beaches	fruit trees	a warm climate
coconut trees	oysters and fish	wild pigs

Write their conversation as they sit on the beach and make plans for exploration and survival. Try to include the contractions of these phrases:

I shall	we are	we have	it is
you will	there is	it will	there is
it has	they are	I have	you are
we cannot	it would	we have not	where is

Remember

Use what you have learned about speech punctuation, too.

Check your progress

LEVEL 4	I can sometimes use apostrophes
LEVEL 5	I can use apostrophes for short forms of words, especially in familiar language and speech
LEVEL 6	I can use a full range of punctuation accurately

3 Use apostrophes for possession

This lesson will

● help you understand how to **use apostrophes to show ownership.**

Using possessive apostrophes correctly means that you can express your ideas more clearly.

Getting you thinking

Look at these sentences and put the apostrophe in the correct place.

This is the dogs collar.
Have you seen the ladies toilet?
I was listening to Mr Davies jokes.

How does it work?

The rules of the possessive apostrophe are simple:

● Put 's or ' on the end of the owner word.
● For **singular** words add 's.
● For **plural** words ending in -s add ' only: *ladies' toilets*.
● For names ending in -s add ' only: *Mr Davies' jokes*.

Most singular owner nouns just add 's:

Britain's Air Force
Cathy's bike
London's streets and squares
a day's work
my sister's boyfriend

Look out for **owner names ending in –s**. You will see them ending in 's or just '. Most people prefer the second choice (although neither is wrong):

Dickens' novels, instead of **Dickens's novels**

The same applies to nouns ending in -s:

bus' wheels

For **plural owner words ending in –s**, just add ':

boys' football match (several boys)
grandparents' anniversary

Words with **–en plural endings** also take 's:

men's snooker club
children's literature

Glossary

singular: one
plural: more than one

Top tips

Don't confuse:
its = belonging to it
it's = it is

Now you try it

Here are ten owner words and ten things owned. Put them together, using the possessive apostrophe correctly.

Hopkins	poems	James	bank account
two weeks	holiday	Mercedes	engine
babies	prams	its	collar
fortnight	time	men	shoe shop
Uncle	birthday		
cars	parking places		

Compare your answers with a partner – did you agree?
Take turns to explain the rule to one another to make sure that you both really understand it.

Development activity

You are writing a chatty letter to a friend. As it is an informal letter, it is fine to use contractions like I've (I have), there's (there is), he's (he is).

In your letter, you are describing the house of a family that you know and recently visited. Include some of the following details about the house:

> Sitting room: large, ugly wallpaper, battered furniture, smell of dogs, very old TV, pictures painted by father
>
> Parents' bedroom: four-poster bed, large cracked mirror, chest covered with make-up jars
>
> Dad (Mr Williams): studio: piles of canvases, table covered with paints, art posters
>
> Twins (Laura and Gemma) (13): bedroom: bunk beds, piles of soft toys, Harry Potter poster
>
> James (17): bedroom: black painted walls, new laptop, clothes lying on floor, dirty dinner plates, desk crowded with folders, Batman poster

Make sure you get all the apostrophes, whether for contraction or possession, exactly right!

You could start your letter:

> *I didn't tell you about the sleepover at the twins' house last weekend. You won't believe what happened...*

Check your progress	LEVEL 4	I can sometimes use apostrophes
	LEVEL 5	I can use apostrophes for possession
	LEVEL 6	I can use a full range of punctuation accurately

This lesson will
- show you how to use **semicolons**.

Semicolons are used to separate **long lists** of descriptions or ideas.

Getting you thinking

A semicolon (;) **divides**. Look back at a book you have read in class or at home. Find examples of where semicolons have been used.

Compare your examples with a partner. Have you found examples of
- semicolons in lists?
- semicolons linking or contrasting ideas?

How does it work?

A semicolon is used in two particular places:

1 To divide longer items in a **list**.

> The battlefield was a dreadful sight: broken tanks lay half-submerged in mud; mangled corpses had been left in every possible attitude; huge shell holes reflected the lurid sunset; and broken trees pointed at the sky like accusing fingers.

You could use commas, but the semicolons make the sentence easier to follow. With a list like this you always open, or begin, the list with a colon (:).

2 To **contrast** two **statements** that are closely related. If you use a semicolon, no connective is needed.

> Dogs are friendly but need constant attention; cats are independent and easy to manage.

These sentence patterns are very useful in factual notes and essays in all school subjects, or in speeches for a debate. They demonstrate a mature writing style and a logical organisation of thoughts.

Now you try it

Look at the following pairs of contrasting ideas. For each idea, write a single sentence. Then to draw a contrast between the two ideas, put the two ideas into one sentence, using a semicolon to separate the statements.

1	primary school	secondary school
2	city	country
3	films	books
4	football	rugby
5	boy bands	rappers
6	summer	winter
7	war	peace

Development activity

Rupert Brooke wrote 'The Great Lover' in 1914 to explain the little things that he enjoyed in life.

These I have loved:
    White plates and cups, clean-gleaming,
Ringed with blue lines; and feathery, **faery** dust;
Wet roofs, beneath the lamp-light; the strong crust
Of friendly bread; and many-tasting food;
Rainbows; and the blue bitter smoke of wood;
And radiant raindrops couching in cool flowers;
And flowers themselves, that sway through sunny hours,
Dreaming of moths that drink them under the moon;
Then, the cool kindliness of sheets, that soon
Smooth away trouble; and the rough male kiss
Of blankets; grainy wood; live hair that is
Shining and free; blue-**massing** clouds; the keen
Unpassioned beauty of a great machine;
The **benison** of hot water; furs to touch;
The good smell of old clothes; and other such –
…Sleep; and high places; footprints in the dew;
And oaks; and brown horse-chestnuts, glossy-new;
And new-peeled sticks; and shining pools on grass; –
All these have been my loves.

Glossary

faery: fairy

massing: gathering, building

benison: a blessing

The semicolons are very much part of the poem's meaning and rhythm.

Now try writing your own list poem about things you love, using the same punctuation pattern.

- Bring in details from your five senses and include up-to-date pleasures.
- Make sure that you use semicolons to divide your ideas.

Check your progress

LEVEL 4	I can use commas in lists
LEVEL 5	I can use semicolons to contrast statements, or to divide longer items in a list
LEVEL 6	I can use a full range of accurate punctuation including semicolons

This lesson will
● help you use colons confidently and correctly.

The colon can be very useful to improve your writing, as long as you use it in the **right places**.

Getting you thinking

A colon (:) **introduces**. It can introduce a list of items or further explanation after a general statement has been made. It is often used in imaginative and factual writing, especially in notes.

Look at some books or magazines you have read. Find examples of where colons have been used.

How does it work?

1 A colon is used to **introduce a list of items**.

● Start with an introductory statement, which should be a complete **sentence**.

● Then add your colon.

● The list, starting with a small letter, then follows.

> **Top tips**
>
> The introductory statement should be a complete sentence. 'In the loft, I found:' is not correct.

In the loft, I found relics of family history: old letters,

　　　　complete clause introduction　　colon　list

faded photos, vinyl records, broken toys, and dusty furniture.

2 A colon is also used in a sentence where **a general statement** is followed by **more detailed evidence** to explain or develop the idea.

Smith was the perfect footballer: he was untiring, passed well,

　　　　general　　　colon　　evidence

evaded tackles easily, positioned himself cleverly and shot powerfully.

The explanation that follows the statement does not have to be long.

I would like to thank the people who have supported me through good and bad times: my mother and father.

Holmes was certain of one thing: the Hound was not supernatural.

Now you try it

1 Here is a general statement:

My closest friends are these people (Add a colon and a list of names.)

Now think of your own sentence like this, including a colon and a list.

2 Here is another general statement:

I have one chief ambition in life (Add a colon and a single phrase or clause.)

Now write your own statement, followed by a colon and a single explanation.

Development activity

Colons are also used in playscripts.

- Put the character's name in the margin (usually in capitals), followed by a colon.
- Then write what the character says.
- You do not need to use speech marks.
- Start the next character's speech on a new line.

> **ALICE:** *(sadly)* He's gone… and I'm afraid I'll never see him again.
>
> **JANE:** *(jumping up and hugging her friend)* London's not so far away. He'll be back. You'll see…

To practise using colons, create your own short play script. You could base this on the following situation or use your own idea:

Anita (15) wants to go to the local nightclub with her friends. Mum is worried and tries to reason with Julie. Dad becomes cross and refuses his permission. Her older brother, Jay, who is just home from university, tries to keep the peace and promises his sister some sort of night out.

As well as using colons to introduce each character's speech, are there any other ways you can use colons or semicolons in this piece of writing?

 Check your progress

LEVEL 4 I can use full stops, commas and some speech punctuation

LEVEL 5 I can use colons to introduce a list or an explanation of a general statement, or in playscripts

LEVEL 6 I can use a full range of punctuation accurately, including colons

73

Level Booster

LEVEL 4

- I can use commas in lists
- I can punctuate and set out written speech
- I can use bracketing commas

LEVEL 5

- I can use more complicated speech punctuation
- I can use apostrophes for contraction and possession
- I can use the colon and semicolon correctly

LEVEL 6

- I can use punctuation for effect
- I can understand the differences between direct and reported speech
- I can avoid common mistakes of grammar and syntax

Chapter 7

AF7 Select appropriate and effective vocabulary

This chapter is going to show you how to

- Use precise vocabulary to make your ideas clearer
- Choose vocabulary that is appropriate for your purpose
- Make effective use of synonyms.

What's it all about?

When you write, your choice of words is probably the single most important thing you can do to make your writing effective. This chapter will help you choose the right vocabulary.

1 Use precise vocabulary to make your ideas clearer

This lesson will
- help you to choose vocabulary to make your meaning absolutely clear.

Whether you are writing to describe, persuade, inform or advise, you need to use vocabulary to help the reader understand precisely what you mean.

Getting you thinking

Look at these two drafts of an opening to a ghost story. In the second draft, the student has worked on the vocabulary to give a clearer sense of how creepy the house is. Has she succeeded?

First draft

Charles walked up the stairs. A cool breeze accompanied the winter sunlight that poured through the open windows. He began to get a bit scared. He looked around, wondering if anyone else was about. The house was shadowy and falling down.

Second draft

The boy crept up the stairs, holding his breath nervously. The ice cold wind whipped through the shattered windows. Shards of glass reflected his terrified expression. He span round in a panic, convinced he was being followed. Shadows seemed to slide across the crumbling, mouldering walls.

How does it work?

The second draft gives a much clearer image of the creepy house.

Notice movements and feelings:

- the boy 'crept' rather than just 'walked' because he was 'nervous' and 'terrified'
- he 'span' rather than 'looked around'
- the shadows 'seemed to slide' as if alive!

Notice details:

- the windows are 'shattered', not simply 'open'
- the 'crumbling, mouldering walls' sound much more sinister than just saying the house was 'falling down'.

Now you try it

Rewrite this opening to a detective story using more precise vocabulary. Try to give the reader a clear idea of the setting and create a mysterious atmosphere.

It was raining and there was lightning. Sir Alec Williams lay dead in a pool of blood. Detective Inspector Lazenby looked around the room for clues. The drawing room curtains were open and the wind was coming through the open window. Wet footprints led from the body to the door and a gun was on the floor.

Think about which

- **nouns** or **verbs** you could change to create a more vivid picture
- **adjectives** and **adverbs** you could use to add detail to your writing.

Development activity

1 Work in a group of four. Using separate sheets of paper, you should each write the opening paragraph of a story. Decide who will write

   a science fiction story

   a spy story

   a romance story

   a story of your own choice.

   Remember to use vocabulary that fits the genre.

2 Everyone should spend five minutes starting their story, then pass it on for the next person in your group to continue. Do this four times until everyone has written part of each story. Then read them out loud.

   - Discuss the vocabulary used in each one and whether the choices made were suitable for the genre.
   - Then, together, pick out examples of strong writing and decide on improvements for weaker spots. What new verb, noun, adjective and adverb choices could you make to improve the writing?

Glossary

nouns: things, people, places or ideas

verbs: doing or being words (I **am**, he **runs**)

adjectives: words that describe a noun (the **fat** cat)

adverbs: words that describe a verb (he runs **quickly**)

Top tips

Use a thesaurus to find alternative words (but also use a dictionary to check the word matches your meaning).

Check your progress

LEVEL 4	I can use words to make my work easy to understand
LEVEL 5	I can use a range of vocabulary to make my ideas clear
LEVEL 6	I can use an ambitious range of vocabulary to express my ideas with clarity and precision

2 Choose vocabulary that is appropriate for your purpose

This lesson will
● help you match your choice of words to the purpose of your writing.

You need to be able to select words that fit the **purpose of your writing**.

Getting you thinking

In the following letter, a student is trying to persuade his headteacher to ban homework! In the second draft he has tried to make the vocabulary more persuasive.

First draft

Homework isn't fair. We work all day at school and are then expected to go home and work all night there as well. Young people should be encouraged to find ways to amuse themselves: joining clubs, reading books or watching films. This will improve their understanding of people and also help them to relax because life isn't all about homework.

Second draft

Homework is unjust. We toil all day at school and are then pressured to return home and slave away all night there as well. Young people should be encouraged to seek out ways to amuse themselves: enrolling in a club or appreciating the arts. This will improve their understanding of people immensely and also ensure that they relax. Life is too precious to poison with homework.

● With a partner, discuss how successful the changes made to the vocabulary are.
● Which words make the letter particularly persuasive?

How does it work?

In the second draft, the vocabulary is much stronger and more **emotive**, which helps the student to achieve his persuasive purpose.

Glossary

emotive: designed to produce an emotion in the reader

For example:

- everyday verbs (such as *work*) have been replaced by more emotive alternatives to have more emotional impact on the reader (*toil, slave away*)
- adverbs (such as *immensely*) have been added to make the work more memorable
- adjectives have been replaced by stronger alternatives (so *isn't fair* becomes *unjust*).

Now you try it

Rewrite this speech, trying to use powerful and engaging words to make it more persuasive. Some words and phrases that could be improved have been underlined.

> The <u>idea</u> that we ban mobile phones at school is <u>silly</u>. It would be <u>bad</u> to <u>get rid of</u> something <u>very</u> useful. Mobiles are an <u>important part</u> of our lives: keeping us in contact with our <u>friends and family</u>, as well as <u>keeping us safe</u>. My mum <u>worries</u> and <u>likes me to</u> contact her if I'm going to be late home.

Development activity

Plan and draft an advice sheet for young people about how to live a healthy lifestyle. You could include sections on diet, exercise and how to use your spare time.

- Select your words carefully so that you sound as if you are advising, rather than ordering your reader to do something. For example, *You could...,* *Have you thought about...*

- Make your ideas easy to follow and get them sounding friendly and sensible, so that readers are more likely to follow your advice. For example, *You don't have to join a gym, just choosing to walk or cycle can help you to...*

Top tips

Use connective words that show sequence (such as *firstly, secondly, next, finally*).

Check your progress

LEVEL 4	I can use some words to get different ideas across
LEVEL 5	I can use a range of vocabulary that matches my purpose
LEVEL 6	I can use an ambitious range of vocabulary to create specific effects

79

3 Make effective use of synonyms

This lesson will
- help you vary your vocabulary to make your writing more interesting.

Words that have similar meanings are called synonyms. Using synonyms will stop your writing getting repetitive.

Getting you thinking

Read this extract from the novel *A Handful of Dust* by Evelyn Waugh.

> Outside, it was soft English weather; mist in the hollows and pale sunshine on the hills; the **coverts** had ceased dripping, for there were no leaves to hold the recent rain, but the undergrowth was wet, dark in the shadows, **iridescent** where the sun caught it; the lanes were soggy and there was water running in the ditches.

Glossary

coverts: thickets or woodland

iridescent: shimmering, multicoloured

- With a partner, pick out all the different words associated with **wet** and **light** that are used to create an engaging description of the English countryside.

How does it work?

Waugh uses words like 'mist', 'dripping', 'rain', and 'soggy' to build up an image of the continually wet countryside.

To convey the type of light, Waugh uses 'soft, pale sunshine' and 'iridescent': it's not the blazing hot sun of summer but a cooler, springtime sun that makes everything glitter.

Not all of these words are exact **synonyms** of wet and light ('dripping', 'soggy' and 'sunshine' are), but they all help to build up a vivid picture.

Now you try it

1 With a partner, make a list of other synonyms you could use for 'wet' and 'light'.

2 Now take it in turns to suggest synonyms for each of the words in the box below. If you get stuck, check in the thesaurus.

| nice   dark   ugly   weak   take   small   run   make   large |

3 You can use synonyms in all types of writing, not just describing. Using a thesaurus, find synonyms for the word 'important' to complete this persuasive speech.

I am here to talk about the _____ issue of the environment. It is _____ that we stop polluting the atmosphere and realise how _____ caring for our world really is. A particularly _____ factor in reducing pollution is recycling. We play a _____ role in teaching our children about cutting down waste.

Remember

Choose synonyms with the **exact meaning** you want for your writing. Whether you are using a thesaurus or picking words from memory, you should check your choices in a dictionary.

Development activity APP

1 Imagine you are on holiday. Write a postcard to your partner: one of you should be having a holiday filled with sun and heat; the other should be having non-stop rain and freezing temperatures. Use synonyms to describe to each other how your holiday is going.

2 Now try using synonyms in some informative writing. Complete a report for the police concerning an argument between two neighbours about noise. However, you cannot use the words 'said', 'loud' or 'quiet'. Instead, use lots of suitable synonyms.

Top tips

Try never to use the same word twice in a paragraph – always ask yourself: 'is there a more interesting way I could say that?' or 'how could I put that differently?' This will boost your level.

Check your progress

LEVEL 4 | I can use some synonyms to make my work more varied

LEVEL 5 | I can use a range of synonyms to keep my work varied and interesting

LEVEL 6 | I can use an ambitious range of synonyms that are effective and varied

Level Booster

LEVEL 4

- I can use words to make my work easy to understand
- I can use some words to get different ideas across
- I can use some synonyms to make my work more varied

LEVEL 5

- I can use a range of vocabulary to make my ideas clear
- I can use a range of vocabulary that matches my purpose
- I can use a range of synonyms to keep my work varied and interesting

LEVEL 6

- I can use an ambitious range of vocabulary to bring clarity and precision to my writing
- I can use an ambitious range of vocabulary to create various effects that will meet the purpose of my writing
- I can use an ambitious range of effective synonyms that are engaging and help to make my work stand out

Chapter 8

AF8 Use correct spelling

This chapter is going to show you how to

- Learn to spell words with prefixes or suffixes correctly
- Spell homophones correctly.

What's it all about?

Making sure you use correct spelling in all your writing.

Learn to spell words with prefixes or suffixes correctly

This lesson will
● help you to be accurate in your spelling of words with a prefix or a suffix.

Prefixes and suffixes are groups of letters that are added to the start or end of a word to change its meaning.

How does it work?

Prefixes

1 Prefixes are added to the **beginning** of words to make a new word. For example, 'substandard'.

2 When a prefix ends in -e and the word begins with e, or with the prefix non-, you should include a hyphen after the prefix. For example, re-enter, non-fiction.

3 Another prefix is in- or im-, which means not, for example: informal, imbalanced. You should always use in-, unless the word you are adding it to begins with a letter b, m or p, in which case you use im-.

Now you try it

1 Copy down these prefixes. For each one, come up with a different example from the one in the box. To help you, there is also an explanation of each prefix.

Prefix	Explanation	Example
fore	in advance	forethought
non	not	non-stop
pre	before	precooked
re	again	resubmit
sub	under	submarine
un	(reversal of a word's meaning)	unhelpful

2 Add the correct **in-** or **im- prefix** to the following words. Write down their new meaning afterwards (you might need a dictionary to help you).

correct	edible	fallible	mature	mobile
patient	perfect	polite	sincere	visible

How does it work?

Suffixes

Suffixes are placed at the **end** of words. The changes they make to a spelling are more complex. The most commonly used suffix is '-ing'. It can cause spelling problems. Although there are some exceptions, here are some general rules to help you:

1 If the word ends in an -e, simply replace the -e with -ing.

   For example, take becomes taking.

2 If a word contains a long vowel sound (the ah sound in arm, the ee in sea, the aw in pour, the er in purse, the oo in group) before the final consonant, just add -ing.

   For example, calming, feeling, clawing, hurting, shooting.

3 If a word contains a short vowel sound (the a sound in cat, the i in sit, the o in hot, the u in sun) before the final consonant, double the last consonant and then add -ing.

   For example, trapping, swimming, robbing, cutting.

> **Top tips**
>
> Think of the two words 'hope' and 'hop'. In 'hope' the vowel is long 'oh' and in 'hop' it is short. 'Hope' becomes 'hoping' and 'hop' becomes 'hopping'.

Now you try it

1 Discuss with a partner whether the following words end with a long or a short vowel sound, then add the -ing suffix correctly:

alarm	brake	burn	farm	feel
gnaw	hit	learn	peel	pop
recruit	rip	rot	run	sag
snore	stun	tag	wait	whip

2 One exception to these rules is with the short vowel sound e (as in bed or help). Using a dictionary, check how the spelling changes when you add -ing to the following words:

dread	forget	head	interest	let
relent	set	shed	tread	wed

Check your ogress

LEVEL 4 I can spell words that use the most common prefixes and suffixes correctly

LEVEL 5 I can spell most words that use prefixes and suffixes correctly

LEVEL 6 I can spell words that use prefixes and suffixes correctly

2 Spell homophones correctly

This lesson will
- help you to choose the correct spelling for words that sound the same.

Homophones are words that sound the same but have different meanings and spellings. It is important that you learn to tell the difference between them so that your writing always maks sense.

How does it work?

there / their / they're

These are homophones that often cause spelling problems. Here are the different meanings:

there = place or position (We parked the car over **there**.)

their = ownership (It was **their** car.)

they're = abbreviation of 'they are' (**They're** getting out of the car.)

Now you try it

Copy out this paragraph, correcting the underlined homophones.

I was walking along the street when <u>their</u> was a loud noise. Two boys came running from <u>they're</u> house, <u>there</u> faces full of panic. I asked if <u>they're</u> was anything I could do to help but they just pointed back at <u>there</u> hallway and shouted, '<u>There</u> still in <u>their</u>!'

How does it work?

its / it's and **your / you're**

These pairs of homophones are often confused. Here are the different meanings:

its = ownership, just like his/her (The bird had hurt **its** wing.)

it's = abbreviation of 'it is' (**It's** cold outside.)

your = ownership (Where is **your** coat?)

you're = abbreviation of 'you are' (**You're** going to school.)

Top tips

With these words, always ask yourself, 'is there a letter missing? What does this word really mean?'

Now you try it

Look at these pairs of homophones. Use a dictionary
if you need to, to check the different meanings of
both words in each pair. Write a sentence using each
pair of words.

hear / here	no / know	one / won
sea / see	to / too / two	wear / where

Development activity

1 Rewrite this paragraph, filling in the blanks with the
correct homophones from the list above.

> She liked _____ stand by the _____ and _____ the
> sound of the waves. If it was _____ cold, she would
> _____ a fur coat she had once _____ at cards. _____
> or _____ people would _____ her and acknowledge
> her curiously: _____ one seemed to _____ her, or
> _____ she lived.

2 Now proofread the paragraph below and change any of
the homophones that have been used incorrectly.

> I couldn't bare to see him – couldn't even stand the site
> of him. He'd been so shore of himself; thinking that he
> was sum kind of hero, but I new the truth. Their had just
> been the too of us there hanging around in the
> newsagent. I was looking for some suites to by, but I
> didn't realise that he was busy steeling stationery. It was
> only when wee started to leave that the shop-owner
> shouted, 'Weight! Your not going too leave without buying
> those things are you?' I turned and staired at him. Then I
> turned on my tale and ran.

LEVEL 4	I can spell most common words but confuse words that sound the same
LEVEL 5	I can spell common words and most homophones correctly
LEVEL 6	I can spell most words, including complex vocabulary

Check
your
ogress

Level Booster

LEVEL 4

- I can spell most common words but confuse words that sound the same
- I can spell plurals but have some trouble with other word endings

LEVEL 5

- I can spell common words and most homophones correctly
- I can use prefixes correctly and use suffixes to spell the endings of most words correctly

LEVEL 6

- I can spell most words, including complex vocabulary
- I can use suffixes to spell the endings of complex words correctly

Teacher Guide

Where the final task of the double-page section is substantial enough to provide a snapshot of students' progress, this has been marked as an **APP opportunity**.

Each double-page section ends with a **Check your progress** box. This offers a levelled checklist against which students can self- or peer-assess their final piece of writing from the **Development** or, occasionally, **Now you try it** section.

The end of chapter **Level Booster** is a less task-specific checklist of the skills students need to master to reach Level 4, 5 and 6. It can be used to help students see the level they are working at currently and to visualise what they need to do to make progress.

To the Teacher

The general aim of these books is the practical and everyday application of **Assessment for Learning (AfL)**: to ensure every child knows how they are doing and what they need to do to improve. The specific aim is to support **APP (Assessing Pupils' Progress)**: the 'periodic' view of progress by teacher and learner.

The books empower the student by modelling the essential skills needed at each level, and by allowing them to practise and then demonstrate independently what they know and can do across every reading and writing (APP) strand. They help the teacher by providing opportunities to gather and review secure evidence of day-to-day progress in each **Assessment Focus (AF)**. Where appropriate (and especially at lower levels) the books facilitate teacher **scaffolding** of such learning and assessment.

The series offers exercises and examples that we hope will not only help students add descriptive power and nuance to their vocabulary but also expand the grammatical constructions they can access and use: above all, the ability to write and read in sentences (paragraphs, texts) – to think consciously in complete thoughts. We aim at fuller, more complex self-expression – developing students' ability to express themselves simply or with complexity and the sense to choose when each is apt.

Each AF is a provisional isolation of various emphases, to be practised and mastered before bringing it back to the real reading and writing (of whole texts) in which all these – suitably polished – skills can be applied.

Gareth Calway

Series Editor

1 Capture your reader's interest and imagination

Students will need access to the library or internet for the final part of this lesson. Alternatively, bring a range of appropriate books and print outs about slavery (particularly the Middle Passage) to class for students to look at.

Getting you thinking

Read the extract aloud to the class, helping them with any unfamiliar vocabulary.

You may want to contextualise the passage, by sharing some of the key facts about slavery and the slave trade.
http://www.understandingslavery.com/teachingslavetrade/introduction/keyfacts/

http://www.primarycolours.net also contains some useful teacher resources.

Now you try it

Students are initially aiming to write around two hundred words at most. The key point is for them to imagine what the experience would be like, and to put themselves in the mind of a child who has been separated from his or her family and taken off into a terrifying, completely unfamiliar environment. The ship would be the climax of a long series of such misfortunes.

Students could start by jotting down one idea or image for each of the senses, then draw on these notes when they come to write their first draft.

Development

Some useful websites to direct students towards might be

http://www.liverpoolmuseums.org.uk/ism/slavery/middle_passage/

http://www.diduknow.info/slavery/

http://www.understandingslavery.com/teachingslavetrade/

http://www.bbc.co.uk/history/british/abolition

http://www.guardian.co.uk/uk/interactive/2008/oct/13/black-history-month-timeline

2 Choose the right type of text

Showing students a variety of the different types of text will help them to understand the context in which each would be used. A couple of clear examples will also help them appreciate the importance of writing appropriately for purpose and audience.

For example, if students wanted to tell a friend about a surprise birthday party, they would probably write an email or text message. However, if they were writing to complain about something to the local council, they would be more likely to write a formal letter.

Getting you thinking

Once the students have discussed the alternative types of writing, in pairs, ask a few pairs to feed back to the rest of the class.

How does it work?

You could show the students examples of the different kinds of writing. Class discussion – how does each make them feel? What kind of words do they use? How does the tone of each differ?

Now you try it

Read through the poem 'The Sorrows of Yamba' with the class, and check their understanding. D they find the poem moving? Would it persuade someone to support the abolition of the slave trade?

You might like to brainstorm ideas from the poem and the picture that students could use as basis for their own piece of writing. Students could also look back at the Olaudah Equiano extract on the previous pages.

Development

The websites suggested for Lesson 1 will also be useful here.

Getting you thinking

1 Read through the extract with students. Explain that they need to pick out the most important information first: where the accident is, what has happened, who is involved, whether an ambulance should be called.

2 If necessary, remind students of the various methods that can be used to create a plan and make sure they are clear about what each one is. Explain that there is no 'right' method to use and that different people find different methods suit them. The key thing is to pick out the important information and to present it in the right order. Some methods are more helpful for particular tasks, though. For instance, a numbered list or a flow chart will be more helpful than a spider diagram if you are trying to put information in a logical order.

How does it work?

Share these examples with students, to help explain the different approaches.

The following call was recorded at the time:

> Hello, yes – oh my God – I need an ambulance now… yes, on the road up to the Corbenic Estate – it needs to be where all this accident and stuff is happening… where the roads go round and there are five different roads going off in every direction…

But the event was reported in writing like this:

> An ambulance was called to the RTA/possible crime scene at the Fiveways roundabout on Corbenic Way.

Now you try it

Encourage students to add as much detail and information as they can, as they extend their plan.

Development

An extension activity for students who finish early or for more able students:

- How would this accident be reported in a local newspaper?
- What different details might be included?
- How would the way the report is organised be different?

  Discuss your ideas with a partner. Then plan and draft a front-page newspaper report about the accident.

Remind students that newspaper articles have to get to the point quickly. Their first paragraph must include the facts – Who? What? Where? Why? When? – before they go on to discuss the story.

Write vividly, powerfully, precisely

Getting you thinking

This lesson encourages students to make imaginative – yet concise – word pictures by first asking them to draw actual pictures in response to some poetic images.

How does it work?

Draw out with students that the two poetic descriptions concentrate on the image. They cut out filler phrases like *There was… I looked up above… which was…*

Help students to see that

A uses a **simile** to compare the autumn moon to a red-faced farmer. The picture of the moon leaning towards you as it appears over a hedge is clear, precise and strong.

B uses an **extended metaphor** to compare a green sea crashing over the shore with a forest blowing in the wind, **or** to compare a fir tree blowing in a wind to the sea's waves.

- The **precise word choices** – 'hurl', 'whirl' – tell us a great deal in a short space.

Explain to students that, in the same way, choosing striking words and images and cutting out 'filler' phrases will help them create powerful writing. They want their reader to absorb every word and not 'skim read' because they are bored!

Now you try it

Make it clear to students that the person they have strong feelings about can't be anyone in the room and that they must keep the person's identity secret. Students can then have great fun with this activity. Other ideas to get students to generate images include: a city, a month, a colour, an animal, a vehicle, a kitchen utensil, an article of clothing.

5 Develop a clear and convincing voice

Getting you thinking

Read the extract aloud and discuss the questions as a class. Also ask them:

- Why do they think Kevin Brooks chose to write in the first person?
- How does this help us get a picture of Martyn's thoughts and feelings?

How does it work?

You can help make sure students understand the effects of careful word choice in the first person by looking at the short sentences Martyn uses to complain about Alex's lateness (*I'm never late for anything...*). Draw out with students that he comes across as very precise (choosing his words carefully) and well organised; someone who likes to have everything just so.

Now you try it

Encourage students to spend time creating and developing the character of Alex before they start planning. They should pick up all the clues they can find in the extract first. Explain that careful thought and planning now will make their writing much easier and more effective later.

> ## Chapter 2 AF2 Produce texts which are appropriate to task, reader and purpose

1 Make the purpose of your writing clear

Getting you thinking

Read the letter with the class. If they were David Tennant, would they want to come and help? Ask students to pick out any techniques used that they think are effective. Why do they think the school had decided to approach David Tennant?

How does it work?

Take students through the explanation of some of the techniques used.

- Can they find examples to illustrate how the letter is 'polite, formal but also flattering'?
- Can they find the rhetorical question in the first paragraph? ('Wouldn't it be wonderful if the special powers of the Tardis were true?')

Brainstorm ideas as a class. Encourage students to see how the letter stays focused on its purpose throughout.

Development

Suggest different types of charities to students; for instance, a charity for elderly people, a charity to support an elephant sanctuary in Africa, a charity helping people train for the Olympics. Does the nature of the charity alter in any way how they would style their letter? Would it influence which celebrity they would invite?

2 Use appropriate techniques in your writing

Students will need a dictionary during this lesson.

Getting you thinking

If students are stuck for characters to talk about, suggest some famous characters they might know about – Harry Potter, any of Roald Dahl's characters, a character from a book they have recently been enjoying in class, even characters from fairy tales. You could give them some books they may be familiar with to help them.

How does it work?

Go through the list with the class and invite students to give some examples of the techniques listed. Write some examples on the board.

Now you try it

Read the whole extract with the class, and ask students for their impressions of the main character. Then read it through again, maybe a section at a time. Students could put their hand up as they come across a writing technique. Encourage students to look for any additional techniques to the ones listed, too. For example, what do they notice about the length of the paragraphs? What is the effect?

Development

Students should aim to write about 200 words here. The image is there as a stimulus but some students may prefer to develop a character of their own. They should be thinking about who the character is, what they do, whether they are friendly or not (and other personality traits), where have they been or where are they going, etc.

Remind them that good writers will show or reveal a character's personality through the character's actions rather than telling us about it directly. For example, instead of saying, 'Dan hated his Science lessons', they could say, 'Dan looked at his timetable and sighed. Slowly he made his way towards the Science lab'.

As extension activities, students could

- Research other effective descriptions of characters. They could then add to their list of techniques and devise a top ten tips for describing characters.

- Observe a friend or family member and try to write a short description of them using only their observation, not any other information they know.

- Do some dictionary and thesaurus work. Many developing writers use dull vocabulary. Find more interesting words for the following words: nice, brown, outgoing, quiet, bad.

- Ask their partner to look at their piece of writing and highlight the three best sentences. They should then ask the partner to tell them where they could have made it better. Ask them to be specific about words and sentences. Students should revise their work in the light of their partner's comments.

Maintain a clear viewpoint in your writing

First, make sure that students understand fully what is meant by a writer's **viewpoint**. Ask them to think of as many examples as they can of types of writing where it is important to develop a viewpoint. Explain that expressing a clear viewpoint helps make writing much more lively and interesting.

Help them to see that different texts require different kinds of viewpoint. For example, if they were writing a newspaper report of a football match, they might need to keep an objective viewpoint to present a balanced account of the game. In contrast, if they were writing about the same match on their own blog, they would probably want their own opinion and support for the team to come through strongly.

Getting you thinking

Ask different students to read each article aloud. Which article or viewpoint do students agree with? Can they explain why?

How does it work?

The first article presents the Food Champions scheme in a positive light. The writer expresses this viewpoint through

- his choice of **adjectives** to describe the scheme ('**brilliant** idea')
- his choice of **verbs** to describe what the Food Champions will do ('**visit** homes', '**advise** people').

He also **selects and orders facts** to present his viewpoint persuasively:

- the article starts by saying £8 billion of food is wasted every year
- the article ends by saying the scheme will help householders save money too.

The second article presents the new scheme in a negative light. The writer

- uses words such as 'nannying' and 'food police' to describe the Food Champions
- does not mention the £8 billion of food wasted each year until later in the article .
- says nothing about helping people or saving them money. Instead he begins by saying people will be 'quizzed' as if they have done something wrong.

Now you try it

Read the article together as a class.

Help students to plan their article by suggesting they might wish to include the following arguments.

- Cats are good because they kill rats, mice and other vermin.
- Cats are good pets (give reasons why).
- Introducing deadly diseases as a method of control might have other consequences.

4 Adapt information and use techniques to suit your purpose

How does it work?

Explain to students that the first text is an encyclopaedia entry. Most students should be familiar with websites like Wikipedia. The text presents a series of factual statements about Brighton, written in a neutral way to inform the reader. Ask students why they think it might be important for encyclopedia-type texts to be neutral in this way.

The second extract is persuasive. It presents the same information but in a different way.

For example, the writer uses

- adjectives such as 'elegant', and positive verbs such as 'enjoy', to make visiting Brighton seem appealing
- a metaphor ('the labyrinth of shops and cafés') to make it sound as if there are so many shops and cafés you could be lost for choice.

Development

Explain to students that, as they are writing a fiction story, they can add extra information and make things up to flesh out the story. Here, the first text is just used for inspiration. It does not need to be 'adapted' in such a literal and faithful way.

However, they should think about story conventions and writing techniques, such as

- having an exciting opening that hooks the reader
- building suspense
- creating vivid description with well-chosen verbs, nouns, adjectives and adverbs.

Will they keep some of the report writer's original word choices, such as 'buzzed' or 'blacked out'? Which descriptions could they expand on?

Chapter 3 AF3 Organise and present whole texts effectively, sequencing information, ideas and events

1 Structure your writing clearly

It would be a good idea to have a range of different comic strip stories for students to compare. Ask them to bring in some of their favourites!

This lesson focuses on a story told in a comic strip format, as the reduced number of words (or lack of words, in this case) means that the writer has to structure the story (and the sequence of frames) very clearly so that the reader can easily follow what is happening. The activities are designed to help students understand the importance of planning and structuring their work carefully, thinking about what they will show or tell the reader at each point in the text.

Getting you thinking

Spend some time asking a number of students to read their description of the events in the comic strip, so that they can see how – even if the words and style used may be fairly different – the sequence of events is clear.

How does it work?

Talk through some different structures for different types of writing and remind students that the best structure to choose depends on the purpose of the writing.

Now you try it

Allow any students who are short of ideas for a storyline to look through some other comic strip stories.

Explain that they should start by planning a simple storyline then divide it up into a series of frames that will make the key events clear. Stress that artistic style is not important – stick figures would be fine.

Development

Students now transfer the clear structure of their comic strip to a plan for a brief talk. They should see that the same principles are involved.

- Plan carefully to start with.
- Make sure your ideas follow clearly and logically.
- Decide how the ideas can be linked together.
- Add details and embellishments to make it interesting or funny.

2 Build your ideas across a piece of writing

Students are now going to consider how ideas can be sustained and developed through a longer piece of writing. The key is to remain focused on your purpose.

Getting you thinking

Allow students to work in pairs on reading the text and answering the questions. This also gives you the opportunity to walk round and check that all students are working along the right lines.

Explain how the writer creates a powerful sense of the setting and the extreme heat. Show them how the heat builds up gradually from 'powerful waves' to 'burning heat' to the 'stifling heat [that] seemed to surge'.

The writer also uses linking words and phrases to show how the heat builds during the day, such as 'The next morning' and 'An hour later'.

Now you try it

Remind students to link their sentences so that the piece develops and shows how their ideas are building.

You could write the following words and phrases on the blackboard to help them.

First of all… Later that day…
It was nearly midday when…
At the end… Firstly…
Secondly… Some time had passed when…
It was only a matter of time before…

Development

Encourage students to talk within their group about how each story or account was built up. Could anything have been added or taken away?

You could ask for volunteers who feel particularly happy with their account to share it with the rest of the class.

3 Improve and extend your presentation skills

Remind students of the importance of presentation as part of the range of techniques that can be used to achieve their purpose in writing. Presentation can be used to draw the reader in as well as to get the key message across as clearly as possible.

Different devices and features are used for different types of text. A rock concert, for example, might use appealing pictures and bright colours, but in a campaign against drink driving, colours might be more sombre.

How does it work?

Feed back students' ideas about who the Animal Aid leaflet is aimed at. They have probably realised the leaflet is aimed at young people of their own age. Draw out with them that we can tell this from the

- **fonts** – the glowing and shattered fonts look edgy and modern, designed to appeal to a young audience.
- **colours** – vibrant and bright, possibly green to suggest nature.
- **pictures** – the image of a cute rabbit makes you want to protect it (but it isn't gruesome or upsetting, showing actual animal torture); the image of an attractive young teen makes Animal Aid look 'cool'.
- **headings** – tell the reader what the leaflet's purpose is (to persuade them to join Animal Aid).

They may also have worked this out from the

- **language** – lots of exclamation marks, use of text language ('4' instead of 'for'), very simple and easy to understand with lots of commands.

- **content** – the text on the left-hand page talks about a 'youth group newsletter' and becoming 'a youth contact'.

Now you try it

Briefly discuss with students what sort of key changes would need to be made to make the leaflet appeal to, and be suitable for, a much younger age range.

Development

Remind students to keep the leaflet they design appropriate, and not to cause offence. It can still have a relaxed and informal style.

4 Organise narrative writing effectively

Getting you thinking

Go through the three-part structure as a class, explaining to students what each stage entails.

As a quick starter, ask students to discuss in pairs a film they have seen recently, or a book they have just read. Does its plot fit the three-part story structure?

Discussing the structure of their film or book should help students to see that, however complex a narrative might initially seem, it can usually be stripped down to the three-part structure.

Read through the extract with the class. It is probably best if you read it aloud to them. Make sure they understand all the language, then discuss which part of the story this probably comes from.

How does it work?

Feed back students' ideas and explain that this extract is taken from the middle of the story. The story is still exciting. It makes you want to read on.

Point out that the middle of a story is where the main action takes place. This is often a conflict or problem (a mystery to be solved or a challenge for a character to overcome). Something crucial

happens that will affect the rest of the story. There can be several conflicts in a novel, to move the story along. The 'Walk of Death' is just one of many conflicts in the book *Tribes*.

It might be useful here to return to the films and books students discussed earlier. Did any students discuss a film or book that they thought had several different storylines, or conflicts to be resolved? Were there any elements that remained unresolved at the end? Explain that this might be to encourage the viewer or reader to use their own imagination about how they were resolved – or, with a film, might even be a 'trailer' for a sequel.

Tell students that a mistake that many would-be writers make is to allow the middle of the story to sag.

Now you try it

Remind students to spend some time planning the beginning, middle and end of their story.

Development

Share some of students' stories with the group. Can the class guess what will happen next?

If appropriate, allow students to write the start and end of their stories.

5 Make your ending link back to your opening

Getting you thinking

Once pairs have read through and discussed the article, ask for feedback and discuss with the class how the article is structured. What important points are included? This is probably best done going through it paragraph by paragraph.

How does it work?

Concentrate here on looking at how the ending links back to the opening.

Now you try it

Show students some examples from local newspapers. Some ideas would be helpful too – school toilets, canteen food, change of uniform policy, a four-day week, for example.

This activity really brings together all the key points that students have been looking at in this chapter.

Remind students how to set out a formal letter.

Development

Here, students can bring in what they have learnt about presentational devices, as well as creating effective persuasive texts.

Chapter 4 AF4 Construct paragraphs and use cohesion within and between paragraphs

1 Use paragraphs in fiction

Examples of blurbs on the back cover of books will be useful later in the lesson.

Getting you thinking

Read the extract to the class. What effect does each part have on the students?

How does it work?

This summarises the principle reasons for starting a new paragraph. Which of the reasons can students spot in the extract from *Thursday's Child*?

Now you try it

This offers students the opportunity to do a similar activity with a later extract from the same novel.

The original layout of the passage is as follows:

> From my place lying on the floor before the fire, I did not need to look up to know Da's eyes had darted to me.

'It was Tin, Mam,' I said listlessly.

'Ah!' Da exclaimed, and his hand slapped the table.

'What do you mean, it was Tin?'

'Harper, enough!'

I crooked my neck to peer at him. 'We have to tell, Da. People are asking.'

Development

Encourage students to try out all the different reasons for starting a new paragraph in their story.

2 Link ideas within and between paragraphs

Getting you thinking

Read the extract with the students before they discuss in pairs. Then ask for feedback about how they think the links and connections are made between the paragraphs.

How does it work?

Allow students to read through this in pairs and to refer the explanations back to the extract. Make sure they are clear about all the links the writer has used before they go on to draft their own short story.

Now you try it

Students are given the sequence of events in a story, so that they can concentrate on their paragraphs and linking techniques without having to worry about the content. They can, of course, add in further details if they wish.

Make sure they also remember to follow a narrative structure and to link the ending back to the opening.

Development

This extends students' work to a different type of text, the blurb on a book jacket. Students will probably find it helpful to look at a range of different blurbs before they start to create their own.

3 Use paragraphs in non-fiction texts

Getting you thinking

This section looks at the use of paragraphs in an argumentative text, which can be more complex. Students need to be clear that such a text will often refer to both sides of the argument and that there is a choice to be made between going through all the arguments on one side first, then the other, or alternating between the two. They will probably find it easier to adopt the former approach but they should be aware of the latter.

How does it work?

Help students to relate the four bulleted points to the extract. Ask whether they think it is effective as an argumentative piece, and why.

Now you try it

The proposal that students are arguing about – that the driving age should be lowered to 14 – is likely to appeal, but obviously students could undertake the same activity with regard to any proposal that interests them.

4 Sequence paragraphs to give information effectively

Students will need access to the library or the internet for the final activity in this lesson.

Getting you thinking

If necessary, explain to students what a flow-chart is by modelling one on the board.

How does it work?

Go over each paragraph, taking suggestions from the class.

- The text starts with a paragraph explaining why it is a good idea to have a qualified instructor.
- The next paragraph gives more reasons for having proper lessons.
- The following paragraph talks about fear and how to overcome it by having a proper instructor.
- The next paragraph describes finding your lead foot.
- The final paragraph encourages the reader to book a lesson.

Now you try it

Students might notice that the penultimate paragraph seems to go off on a different tack from the rest of the article.

Development

How they order and arrange their text will depend on the exact purpose of their advice sheet. Ask students to consider:

- Is it to help someone learn how to do something? (Perhaps the advice sheet could be organised as a series of instructions.)
- Is it to persuade someone to try out a new sport? (The advice sheet would need a persuasive and appealing opening paragraph, and a concluding paragraph that returns to this point.)

5 Organise poems using stanzas

Explain to students that stanzas are often called verses. Emphasise that stanzas, like paragraphs, are often used to introduce a new topic, image, event or theme. However, in poems with a set form (such as sonnets or sestinas) the shape and length of stanzas will be predetermined, and the poet will have to 'fit' their content to this shape.

Getting you thinking

Read the poem aloud together as a class, asking individual students to read one stanza each.

Students should then work in pairs to write their sentences. Ask students to note down anything else they notice about the form or shape of each stanza.

How does it work?

Feed back students' ideas and draw attention to the regular rhythm and rhyme scheme.

Development

Students could work in pairs to do this activity, discussing where and why they choose to break lines and change stanzas. It might be useful to do this on the computer, giving them the unformed block of text to play around with.

Share and compare the final poems that students come up with. Encourage them to alter or add to the words and images used in their poems, if they would like.

Chapter 5 AF5 Vary sentences for clarity, purpose and effect

1 Turn simple sentences into complex sentences

Getting you thinking

Read the short passage aloud to students, trying not to over-emphasise the boring repetitive style! Ask students for their reaction to it. Can they pinpoint why it's not exciting and attention-grabbing?

How does it work?

If students are not clear about simple and complex sentences, write the first sentence from the passage and the complex version of it on the board so that they can compare directly.

Then write a few more simple sentences on the board and ask for suggestions as to how to make them complex. Students can refer to the subordinating conjunctions in their books if necessary. Write these on the board, emphasising the commas.

Ask students whether they think the simple or complex sentences are more interesting. Explain that it is being able to **vary** the length of sentences that will make their writing more effective.

Development

Students might enjoy doing activity 2 in small groups. Groups could then read their revised passages to the rest of the class.

2 Use subordinate clauses

Ensure students understand the difference between main and subordinate clauses by displaying some complex sentences, and highlighting all the main clauses in one colour and the subordinate clauses in another. Include one sentence that features two or more subordinate clauses.

Saying the individual clauses aloud, to see if they make sense in isolation, will help them. Explain that all clauses must contain a **verb**.

Getting you thinking

Students may need a number of examples to help them understand the concept of a **predicate**. It is also worth taking the necessary amount of time to be sure they understand the difference between a **complex** and a **compound** sentence.

How does it work?

As you move on to relative clauses, it will be helpful to give students lots of examples to illustrate how these clauses add information about people or things. If students understand the concept easily, you could introduce the terminology (**relative clause** and **relative pronoun**); otherwise, this is better omitted.

Development

As an extension, you may want to introduce the concept of **defining** and **non-defining** clauses. Give students the following two sentences:

- The street that I live on is full of trees.
- Some pupils at my school, which is in the next town, won the cross-country last week.

Help them to see how, in the first sentence, 'that I live on' is crucial to the meaning of the sentence. On the other hand, 'which is in the next town' is not important to understanding the second sentence – it merely adds detail.

If appropriate, you may also want to explain the difference between 'who' and 'whom', again using lots of examples. Explain to students that whom replaces him, her or it in the relative clause.

> Alice was wearing her new coat. I saw **her** on the High Street.
>
> Alice, **whom** I saw on the High Street, was wearing her new coat.
>
> Tamer Mustafa is now a famous man. I knew **him** at school.
>
> Tamer Mustafa, **whom** I knew at school, is now a famous man.

3 Vary your sentence lengths and structures

Getting you thinking

Read the extract from *Great Expectations* with the class. What do students notice about the first paragraph?

Once students have discussed, in pairs, the effect of the two paragraphs in the extract, help them to analyse why the contrast is effective.

In the first paragraph, the long sentence goes on for several lines. The subject is 'I' and the verb is 'found out'. Then follows a long list of noun clauses, starting quietly with 'that' and following with the repeated phrase 'and that'. Each 'and that' is like a blow, growing heavier as Pip feels lonelier and building up suspense for the reader.

Then, as shocks, come the two short spoken sentences: 'Hold your noise!' and 'Keep still…!' An escaped convict jumps up and seizes Pip. By varying his sentences like this, Dickens controls the pace and atmosphere of his story.

Now you try it

Students should enjoy this extract from *The Haunted House*. Make sure they understand all the vocabulary. Ask them to say how clearly they can see the house in their minds' eye – what details might they add? They should be able to produce effective writing of their own, following the guidelines.

4 Use connectives and vary the order of clauses

Students will need access to computers and the internet for the final activity in this lesson.

Students should now be able to vary the length and type of sentence they use in their writing. They may, however, still be rather predictable in the connectives they use. This lesson will help them introduce more variety into their writing.

How does it work?

Encourage students to experiment with words. Following the example, can they come up with more sentences where they change the word order to put the emphasis on different parts? This is probably best done as a class, pooling ideas to create different ideas and effects.

Now you try it

Following the class activity, students should be able to work successfully in pairs on these activities.

Development

It would help students to be able to do this activity on the computer, to make it easy for them to edit sentences and move them around.

Students should use the given facts about JK Rowling to create a short author biography.

Encourage them to think about reordering the facts to increase the impact, as well as linking them together and changing the order of the sentences. Remind them that an attention-grabbing opening is vital – how would they achieve this?

5 Use different tenses for effect

Help students through the quite complex descriptions of verbs and model for them how different tenses are formed and used.

How does it work?

You may also want to explain that agreement of subject and verb is very important.

- A **singular** subject must be matched to a singular verb form.
- A **plural** subject must have a plural verb form.

The following examples should help:

A group of us is calling for change.

Two **were** convicted. None **was** to blame.
    plural   singular

Display this version:

A group of us are calling for change.

Explain that the 'us' has confused the writer. The singular subject is actually 'group', therefore the verb should be 'is'.

This may also be a good opportunity to explain the difference between subject and object of a verb: that subjects carry out the action and objects are on the receiving end.

I trapped the savage dog.   The savage dog bit **me**.
(subject)   (object)

Students frequently make a mistake with a double subject or object, so it is worth highlighting this.

My friend and me caught the last bus home.

Dad gave John and I a lift to the judo class.

Help them see the problem with these sentences by leaving out 'My friend' and 'John'. Would they say 'me caught' or 'Dad gave I'?

Development

This poem is excellent at making sure students understand what a present participle is! Encourage them to be as creative as they can in writing their own description, which could be written as prose or poetry.

Remind them that powerful writing is not always about using long lists of **adjectives** or **adverbs**. When they have to use more than one adverb, they should ask themselves: is there a stronger, more effective verb I could use here instead?

Chapter 6 AF6 Write with technical accuracy of syntax and punctuation in phrases, clauses and sentences

1 Use speech punctuation effectively

Getting you thinking

You could write the dialogue on the board without the punctuation and find out what the students know already – for example, do they know where the comma and question marks go?

Now you try it

This is also a good activity to do as a class on the board as students can then correct their own mistakes as they go along.

Development

Encourage students to think about how the signalman reacted. What might the ghost want from him or be trying to tell him?

2 Use apostrophes in informal writing

Getting you thinking

Ensure students understand the difference between 'it's' and 'its', as this is a common source of confusion.

Make sure they are clear that contractions should be used very carefully. They should be avoided in any formal writing, though they can be very effective in informal writing – in particular to make dialogue more realistic.

How does it work?

Students will probably have noticed the number of contractions used in Shakespeare's plays.

3 Use apostrophes for possession

Students often disregard apostrophes and their importance. This lesson will help them to realise how an apostrophe carries meaning and how putting them in the wrong place can alter the meaning of a piece of writing.

How does it work?

Work through the rules of the apostrophe for possession with the class and add more examples until they are clear about the rules. You could put a further 5–10 mixed examples on the board to consolidate students' learning.

Now you try it

Point out to students that explaining something to someone else is the surest way of checking you have really understood it yourself. This is why they are asked to work in pairs to check their answers and explain the rules. Take the opportunity to walk round and listen to their explanations.

4 Use semicolons accurately

Point out to students that if they can use semicolons in their writing, it will really impress!

Now you try it

This activity should help students become more familiar with the use of the semicolon to link two related statements.

Development

Rupert Brooke's poem offers an excellent example of the semicolon used in lists. Ask students if they have heard of Rupert Brooke and explain why he was reminiscing in this way about the things he loved in life.

Point out to students that they can use commas, too, for lighter pauses or divisions in their list poem and tell them their poem can rhyme, like Brooke's, or not. It's up to them.

5 Using colons accurately

Getting you thinking

The more usual use of the colon was touched on in the previous lesson, where it was explained that it must be used to introduce a list divided by semicolons.

Development

This activity reinforces the use of the colon but offers students the opportunity to be more creative in their writing, especially if they produce a play script based on their own ideas.

1 Use vocabulary to make your ideas clearer

Students will need access to dictionaries and a thesaurus later in the lesson.

Getting you thinking

Read the two extracts aloud to the students, or ask for a volunteer to read them. Which do they prefer and why? How does each extract make them feel? Elicit their ideas, then explain the difference between the two further if necessary, and find out from the students if they think she has succeeded.

How does it work?

Build on students' initial ideas as a group. See if any of them have other ideas (they normally do!).

Now you try it

Explain to students that their word choices will affect the sound and pace of a piece of writing. You could mention to students that choosing words that alliterate (start with the same letter) can have a powerful effect. They should try reading their revised passage aloud to test out the new tone and tempo they have created.

Development

Once their stories are complete, students could work together to pick out examples of strong writing and decide on improvements for weaker spots. What new verb, noun, adjective and adverb choices would they make to improve the writing?

Students could share stories they are particularly pleased with, with the rest of the class.

2 Choose vocabulary that is appropriate for your purpose

Getting you thinking

Read the first draft to the class. What do they think? Would it persuade their headteacher to ban homework? What could be done differently/better? Change some of the words on the board. Read the class's creation, then the second draft from the text. What do they think of this new draft?

3 Make effective use of synonyms

Students will need access to a dictionary and a thesaurus.

Now you try it

If students are using a thesaurus, make sure they check their choice of words carefully. You could have some fun illustrating the sort of mistakes that can be made!

1 Learn to spell words with prefixes or suffixes correctly

Students will need access to dictionaries for this lesson.

Development

An extension task to set students:

In pairs, write the words from the lists below on a big sheet of paper using three different coloured pens. Choose one colour for the prefixes, another colour for the suffixes and another colour for the words in the left hand column. Then cut out the words to make small cards. Using the cards, see what new words you can create by adding a prefix or a suffix. Use a dictionary to check your new word exists.

Words		Prefixes	Suffixes
fact	alter	re	able
love	mature	dis	ation
walk	hesitate	un	er
inform	grow		ion
do	charm	im	ing
play	spell	in	
worry	standard	sub	less
similar	wash		
exceptional	concoct		
clear	elect		
regulate	appear		
colour			

2 Spell homophones correctly

Students will need access to dictionaries for this lesson.

Development

Try this extension activity:

Work in groups of three or four. You are going to be playing against everyone else in the class. Your teacher will set a timer. The group to come up with the most homophones in the time limit wins! Try to go right through the alphabet. Some letters are harder than others, although even the letters x and z share a homophone!

For example:

ail	ale
bare	